I'M SORRY I CREMATED YOU

I'M SORRY I CREMATED YOU

FINDING THE FUNNY IN LIFE AND LOSS

JACLYN MICHELLE SMITH

Advantage | Books

Copyright © 2024 by Jaclyn Michelle Smith.

All rights reserved. No part of this book may be used or reproduced in any manner whatsoever without prior written consent of the author, except as provided by the United States of America copyright law.

Published by Advantage Books, Charleston, South Carolina.
An imprint of Advantage Media.

ADVANTAGE is a registered trademark, and the Advantage colophon is a trademark of Advantage Media Group, Inc.

Printed in the United States of America.

10 9 8 7 6 5 4 3 2 1

ISBN: 978-1-64225-949-0 (Paperback)
ISBN: 978-1-64225-948-3 (eBook)

Library of Congress Control Number: 2024916058

Cover and layout design by Matthew Morse.

This publication is designed to provide accurate and authoritative information in regard to the subject matter covered. It is sold with the understanding that the publisher is not engaged in rendering legal, accounting, or other professional services. If legal advice or other expert assistance is required, the services of a competent professional person should be sought.

Advantage Books is an imprint of Advantage Media Group. Advantage Media helps busy entrepreneurs, CEOs, and leaders write and publish a book to grow their business and become the authority in their field. Advantage authors comprise an exclusive community of industry professionals, idea-makers, and thought leaders. For more information go to **advantagemedia.com**.

To those who are caring for their parents,
displaying unconditional love and selflessness,

I see you.

CONTENTS

Acknowledgments 1
Prologue 3

1. Yes, And 9
2. Trust Your Scene Partners 31
3. Embrace Failure and Be Adaptable 43
4. Develop Your Character and Play with Joy 73
5. Take Risks and Live in the Moment 93
6. Be Confident in Your Choices 127
7. Be Affected and Let Go 147

About the Author 175
Contact 177

ACKNOWLEDGMENTS

To my chosen family, my McGees—Corinne, Kim, Lisa, Sara, and Philip—thank you for always being there no matter what. I'm eternally grateful for your unconditional love and the immense joy you bring to my life.

I am embarrassed by the richness of friendships with which I've been blessed. Every single one of my friends who has filled and who continues to fill my life with love and happiness, all my strength comes from you. My gratitude has no end.

Uncle George, Aunt Hope, and John, you've been my rock and the memory keepers of Mom's legacy. Thank you for keeping her alive in my heart.

Laura, Garrett, and Grayson, thank you for the love and for sharing my brother with me in the hardest moments of my life. Lance, we are bound by blood and more importantly by love. I'm always so grateful to have you as my only brother.

Nina, you believed in me when I didn't believe in myself and gave me the crazy courage and confidence to write this book. Thank you.

Adam, your generous gift of this opportunity to share my story with the world, as well as providing a workplace where I can be myself even at the worst of times, is priceless. You're amazing; thank you.

I'M SORRY I CREMATED YOU

Ben, you saw my worth and showed me how to lead with empathy by your example. You make doing the right thing cool. Thank you for being you.

Amanda, my book coach, book doctor, story doula, teacher, and life coach, thank you for showing (not telling) me how to be a writer, for believing in me, and for helping me find my words and my worth. This book would not have been possible without you. You are magic.

To my unbelievably talented editors, Lauren and Elizabeth, for loving my story and helping me bring it to life, thank you.

Matthew, thank you for reading my mind and delivering the pitch-perfect book cover and interior design and for always making me look good.

Corrin, the creative genius, thank you for believing in my book and giving it so much passion and love. I feel so blessed to have your expertise and friendship.

To every single person who works for Advantage | Forbes Books and touched my book in any way and/or offered love and words of encouragement during the process, thank you. It takes a village to publish a book!

Carol, you kept me sane all these years. It's a hard job, and someone had to do it. Thank God it's been you.

To all the kind and compassionate human beings at Theatre 99 who help form the Charleston improv community, thank you for helping me laugh through moments that would have broken me and for seeing the best version of me and helping me become her. Thank you for helping me find my strength and the funny.

Mom and Dad, thank you for giving me a beautiful story to tell, the courage to tell it, and the confidence to find my voice. You were the perfect parents for me, and I will love you always.

PROLOGUE

At only eleven, I wrote a poem called "The Power of You," and it was good. Too good. The first line read, "Always believe in the power of you." My poem moved teachers and parents alike.

That weekend Dad told me to get dressed to go to the mall—music to my preteen ears! I raced up to my room and was back just as quickly, decked out in my favorite jean jacket and jelly shoes, circa 1989. I jumped into the passenger seat of Dad's two-door 1977 Chrysler Cordoba.

At our local mall, the illustrious Town Center, we always parked next to the food court entrance. Was that nature or nurture? Did Dad always park next to the food court because I loved food, or did I love food because Dad always parked next to the food court? Potato, patahto …

I was thrilled to visit the mall, where the closest thing to "natural" was the plastic fruit decorating the Orange Julius kiosk windows. The sugary citrus grandfather of the modern smoothie mingled with the oily goodness of deep-dish Sbarro pizzas. Just crossing the threshold to the food court, I was hit with instant, insatiable hunger pangs.

But Dad took my hand and steered me away from the food court. We scurried past Purrfect Place, my all-time favorite store, where I crafted personalized Hello Kitty buttons to adorn my jean jacket. These buttons were my meal ticket! One day I would be discovered by a powerful designer who would recognize my innate talents and offer me a job. I would become the Doogie Houser—child prodigy—of button making. I'd be fashion designer Doogie.

Dad also knew I was a child prodigy, but he saw my future not in plastic button pins but in … poetry. I don't know which one of us was more deluded. It might have been Dad, who dragged me past all the good shops to the Things Remembered store. It could have been worse; it could have been the Sears automotive department.

For those young things born after the fall of the mall, Things Remembered was a shop full of weirdly blank jewelry, trophies, and picture frames, like a half-baked gift shop. The blank spaces were by design, and Things Remembered did a brisk trade "personalizing" their overpriced offerings using an expensive engraving machine.

Dad proudly presented the salesman with a piece of lined paper ripped straight from my Trapper Keeper. This was the incredible poem that was going to make me the twentieth-century Emily Dickinson.

The Things Remembered salesclerk went back and forth with my dad, reviewing all the options as if negotiating a new car, not engraving his daughter's first masterpiece for posterity. Between thoughts of Hello Kitty, pizza, and soft pretzels, I watched these grown men bounce options back and forth, like a Ping-Pong match of fonts and point sizes.

The conversation ended with Dad's selection of a five-by-seven chunk of glass that nestled into a delicate wooden stand. He chose a beautiful cursive font for the sophisticated young artist's words. Dad was more excited about my poem than I was about my buttons. He beamed; his face literally glowed with pride. The heavens opened, casting a holy light over this moment of utter transcendence at Things Remembered.

PROLOGUE

Gazing up at this giddy grown man, I found what I had been seeking all my eleven years on earth. For the low, low price of a poem and an eighty-dollar plaque, I finally secured my dad's approval. After all these years, I finally pleased my dad. What a thing to remember!

. . .

My poem-on-glass was a centerpiece of family pride for the rest of our lives. Well, my parents' lives. From the wood mantel, nestled against the brick fireplace in our big living room, the poem was a testament to my glorious future as one of the greatest writers in the world, and more importantly a future full of accolades and accomplishments.

Only as I got older did I begin to understand the amount of pressure successful writers endure. It was even longer before I understood the immense pressure that poem put on me. It was pressure I couldn't live up to.

The moment Dad placed that poem on that mantel like an offering on a sacred altar, he dedicated *my* entire life to becoming a writer. It was all he ever talked about. Any minor luck at school prompted him to say, "You should write a story about that, Jaclyn." If another kid was a nasty piece of shit, and I came home crying after school, he would say, "You should write a story about how that made you feel."

It wasn't that I didn't *want* to be a writer. I enjoyed writing. But a career wasn't on my radar growing up, you know, aside from creating custom Hello Kitty buttons. The fact that my dad couldn't understand that and refused to let it go made writing less appealing and ultimately less realistic to me.

His encouragement (harassment) to feed my writing drive did not end after my childhood. When I was a young adult with opinions and experiences of my own, instead of agreeing or arguing like a salesman looking for an "in," Dad encouraged me to speak my mind on paper. If I went on a trip, he encouraged me to write an article about every moment of said trip.

"An article?" I would sigh. "Why would I write an article? Who writes articles? I'm not a writer, Dad."

Depending on how hard he was selling it, my protestations might be punctuated with a comment under my breath akin to, "Get off my ass, Dad," accompanied with a nasally huff and dramatic eye roll. Then I'd bring out my daddy's-girl smile, make peace, and change the subject.

Even after I followed my own career path, Dad persisted: "You should write down all of the details of your training so that you can write about your experience as a new hire and help the training program improve ... Hell, you could be a trainer in the training program! Think of all of the knowledge you would bring! But it all starts with writing about it."

Dad never lost faith in my talent as a writer, even if I'd not tapped it since I was eleven with the poem that led to an engraving. Like the evangelical true believer that he was, his greatest disappointment throughout the years was that I failed to see what he saw in me.

I refused to write about a trip, an opinion, or a job. I refused to write about a house. I refused to write about a mouse. I will never write again. I will never write, Dad-I-Am ... This standoff left Dad in a perpetual state of frustration. He could not let it go, and I would not give in, so the topic left both of us annoyed and dreading the next round.

What Dad would never ever know was his faith was in a false god. His dream of Jaclyn Smith, prolific writer, was based on a horrible lie. More than a lie, a sin—the most sacrilegious sin any writer can commit ... plagiarism.

PROLOGUE

Dad would go to his grave, or in his case, his urn, never knowing that my masterpiece of literature was actually lifted from a library book. I claimed it, and I paid a hefty sentence for that crime. To his dying breath, Dad remained steadfast, never doubting his daughter was more talented than anyone ever knew, especially herself. I never had the heart or the courage to tell him the truth.

In my defense, at age eleven, I could never have imagined Dad would cling to that poem with such hope and pride. One dishonest childhood mistake on a random homework assignment defined my father's image of me and shaped his hopes and dreams for the rest of his life. Had I known that the price of Dad's approval was financed with the compound interest of parental overinvestment, I might have paused.

Taking into account the pressure he put on me and the exponential shame of living, and adjusting for inflation, the actual price of my father's approval was exactly one stolen poem, a lifelong lie, rebellion, shame, guilt, ceaseless pressure, and $210.01 (in 2024 dollars) for the plaque.

Had I understood as a child that I would be ashamed of myself for decades after securing my father's one-time approval, I probably would have quickly come clean about the entire thing. I couldn't understand that, though, because I was eleven, and I didn't know anything but my need to be loved.

It was never my intent to lie, just to get a good grade on my sixth-grade homework. I didn't know how highly the teacher and my dad would value my writing, which was actually just my *handwriting*. Making my dad proud at the same time was just a huge bonus.

Of course, to this day I feel the lingering guilt and shame of stealing a poem, claiming it as my own, and then lying to my dad for decades. To this very moment, this has always been the oldest skeleton hidden in the depths of my very messy closet. So, in an act of self-forgiveness, I say to you, dear reader, behold my skeleton! As penance, I will now produce a piece of writing worthy of my father and the humility to admit: he told me so.

YES, AND …

The "yes" part of "Yes, and …" means you accept and embrace your scene partner's contributions, including their character choices. When your scene partner introduces a new character or character trait, accepting their choices creates a supportive environment for creative collaboration.

JANUARY 8, 2022

"Tom Brady is coming to get me tonight," Dad declares.

He's no longer that bespectacled man who towered over me when I was a little girl. In his hospital bed, thin as a rail, Dad now has the demeanor of a child who believes in the Tooth Fairy even as the other kids on the playground laugh at him.

"Tom Brady?" I inquire. I know not to challenge him.

"Yes, Tom Brady. He is going to be here tonight and beam me to New York City with him, through those ceiling tiles up there." To punctuate the thought, Dad gestures with his set chin, indicating the graying ceiling tiles over his hospital bed. When I don't respond quickly enough, he points to the tiles, emphasizing his point of departure.

This exchange is disconcerting on so many levels. Obviously, Tom Brady is not coming to the Grand Strand Medical Center in Myrtle Beach to get Dad, and it scares the hell out of me to realize that Dad actually believes this to be true. Dad isn't even a Tom Brady fan. Seriously. A few months ago, he couldn't have cared any less about Tom Brady or really anybody who didn't play for the Washington Commanders.

Dad's been here the better part of a week, since his visiting physical therapist found him unconscious, slumped over in his living room recliner and soaked in his own urine.

Once the ambulance got Dad to the hospital, the medical team said, based on his health and hydration levels, Dad wasn't unconscious for too long … probably fewer than twenty-four hours. I try to take comfort that he wasn't sitting alone and unconscious in his own urine for more than a day, while still knowing how long just one day can be. It's all but impossible to take comfort in anything at the moment.

Dad is a patient, and I am a visitor at the very same hospital that treated Mom, who had a massive heart attack and almost died several years ago. Spoiler alert: that's not what did her in.

Both of my parents suffered from dementia, so this Tom Brady announcement, while surprising because of the sudden change of football loyalties, is not my first rodeo. So, rather than poke a stick at an already agitated man, I tell Dad how excited I am about his upcoming trip to New York with Tom.

I want to call bullshit on my dad, but his medical team advises me to just go along with his delusion for now. To not agitate him further. So, I ask him to bring me something cool back from the trip, like he always used to do when I was a little girl. Dad rolls his eyes at me and my selfish request. His look alone tells a story: he and Tom have serious business to accomplish in New York and won't have time to shop for an I Love New York coffee mug. Besides, the mug will dissolve when Tom beams him back to his room through the ceiling tiles in time for his dinner.

Honestly, the absurdity and the fear are just part of this complicated tableau. I'm also reveling in the fact that we are having any conversation at all because Dad has spent most of the past few days just lying in his bed, staring at a framed family photograph I brought from his house. There we all are, in that nicked, silver-plated frame, dressed in our elegant evening wear, on a better day, in this treasured photograph. Our whole family gathered at Uncle George and Aunt Hope's wedding many years ago. This photograph radiates so much happiness and hope from a happier and much more hopeful time.

Now, Dad just stares at it in silence for hours upon hours. Trying to break the terrible silence and tension, I offer to feed Dad a cup of chocolate pudding from his dinner tray. Chocolate pudding is about the only thing he will eat now. Dad shakes his head grumpily and says, "God dammit, Jaclyn, I don't want any pudding."

I step out and slow-walk the halls of the hospital, the sanitized walls my only support, breathing the stale hospital air in and out, counting in my head how many days I've been here ... four? Yes, I've been here for four days, sitting and milling around in the same hospital caregiver uniform—my old sweats and sneakers.

Beyond the automatic front doors of the Grand Strand ER, the cold air hits my face hard. I am ecstatic to be outside those hospital walls. Finding my car, I climb inside, lean my head against the headrest, and close my eyes. I long to take a nap, but I know I can't stay out here that long. I also know I am much too stressed to rest. Since I'm here, I grab my nicotine vape pen and take a couple of puffs.

I'M SORRY I CREMATED YOU

Even though I'm a grown woman, I find myself looking around to make sure nobody sees me vaping. I despise my vaping habit, but I've smoked on and off my entire life, since I was fifteen years old. I don't know how to handle this peak adulthood crisis of elderly parent care without it.

Even before this crisis, our relationship had been strained for the last couple of months. With his physical health failing, I did not want him living alone any longer in his home. I was afraid of what would happen to him, but he'd refused to listen to me. He drew a line in the sand that I could not cross. It was his decision to stay in his home and not come live in the assisted living facility I found for him in Charleston.

The facility costs would have been mostly covered by the US Department of Veteran Affairs (VA), so he wouldn't have had to struggle with that part of it. His refusal to consider my proposal caused me to take a big step back from his life.

We hadn't been speaking regularly because I simply couldn't watch him live the way he was living. I couldn't be a part of it. I couldn't condone or contribute to his decline. At that point I was receiving regular phone calls from the Surfside Beach Police Department, who were also concerned for his safety, most often while I was at work. The situation with Dad was causing me so much stress and constant worry that it was starting to affect my job and my health. To save myself, I told Dad a few months before he was hospitalized that I was no longer going to be involved in his life. That was one of the hardest things I'd ever done and to be snapped back into his life under these circumstances is too much.

His first couple of days in the hospital, Dad was completely out of it, barely speaking. He just lay in his bed in a catatonic state. The moment Dad was wheeled into the emergency room, the doctors deployed every test they had in their arsenal. Four days later, it is still unclear what is causing his confusion and escalation to insane hallucinations of Tom Brady.

To find myself here in the ER, to learn he was physically combative with the paramedics, to learn he had to be sedated, it is all too much. Hearing about it secondhand breaks my heart into a million pieces. Dad can be very difficult at times and even verbally combative occasionally but never physically combative.

When Dad woke up from sedation, he had no recollection of what had happened or why he was at the hospital. He was admitted into the hospital for transient global amnesia, a rare form of amnesia that causes sudden memory loss. They settled on this particular diagnosis because the paramedics and doctors had no idea what was truly causing his condition, but every patient needs a label upon which the medical-industrial complex can append its billing codes.

The day before his Tom Brady visit, Dad received both a CT scan and an MRI to determine whether or not he had suffered a stroke. I waited all day in Dad's hospital room, alone, for the results as Dad lay quietly in his bed. The doctor finally came into Dad's room around five in the evening and told me that Dad had not had a recent stroke, though the CT scan and MRI did show that he'd had a handful of minor strokes in the past and he hadn't even realized it.

She explained that a history of minor strokes was not uncommon for someone Dad's age of seventy-eight years. Because his current condition was not stroke related, they'd done more tests; these showed no cranial abnormality or concerns of any kind to indicate a fall, concussion, fracture, or brain tumor. His blood was being tested each day, and no signs of infection were present.

Despite not knowing the exact cause or the full extent of Dad's condition, it was clear to the medical staff that it was severe. So severe that the doctor told me that my brother, Lance, should probably come from Atlanta.

I had been in touch with Lance often over the last few days, since Dad entered the hospital, calling or texting him each time a new test was being performed on Dad and each time I received any kind of update on his condition. When talking to Lance on the phone, I struggled to shove back all the resentment I felt rising up from deep in my stomach.

I was entirely alone at the hospital with Dad. I was the only one available to handle most of Dad's medical, emotional, and physical needs over the last several years, just as I had been the default person to handle most of Mom's needs for many years before she died. I resented that I was doing it all over again for Dad and feeling so alone.

I could hear the pity in Lance's voice and an undercurrent of frustration with the entire situation. The morning of the fourth day, he assured me he'd be making the trip to Myrtle Beach the following day to give me a little reprieve from being at the hospital. I was relieved by Lance's offer but also ambivalent: I'd convinced myself I was the only one who could handle this situation. I was always there to handle Dad's situations. What would happen if I weren't?

On my way back from the parking lot, I inspect the artwork on the hospital walls as I slowly make my way back up to Dad's fourth-floor room. Most of the paintings are beach scenes and landscapes, which makes sense since we are in Myrtle Beach. Near Dad's room, I stop to look at one of the paintings more closely.

A woman in a gigantic straw hat is frolicking with her little girl on the beach. The watercolor painting is beautiful, and the subjects smile and happily gaze into each other's eyes. I stare at the painting, wishing so badly I were on that beach with my mother at that very moment, or really anywhere other than this hospital.

JANUARY 9, 2022, 1:00 P.M.

When Lance arrives, a wave of gratitude washes over me when we hug. This is what it feels like to *not* be alone. This companionship, more than the reprieve, is what I've ached for all these days. Dad is asleep, so I debrief Lance: Dad has refused to eat and is growing weaker with each missed meal. If he continues to refuse food, we'll need to discuss a feeding tube.

His resistance to eating motivated me to stop at Baskin-Robbins to get Dad a scoop earlier the same day Lance arrived. He loves rainbow sherbet almost as much as butter pecan. But would he choke on the pecans? The last thing I need is to kill Dad with pecans. What a freaking death! Or maybe it is the perfect way to go? I guess I wouldn't mind leaving this world eating ice cream ... And so they went, these buzzing thoughts plaguing me for days on end.

Returning to Dad's side, I thought I'd found a surefire way to get him to eat. I proudly revealed the sherbet. Dad looked up at me with the slightest twinkle in his eye. I grabbed a plastic spoon from his table and began feeding him.

His initial excitement and enjoyment lasted a few bites before he lost interest and curled back into his bed. Standing there holding the full cup of ice cream, I contemplated eating it myself. How could I waste ice cream? Yet, I had no appetite. So, I tossed the melting sherbet in the trash, fighting back the tears welling up in my eyes.

JANUARY 9, 2022, 8:00 P.M.

Since I moved to Charleston twenty-three years ago, I've been a huge fan of improv comedy through regularly attending shows at Theatre 99, the local improv theater. After dreaming of taking classes for more than two decades, I finally signed up for the level 1 improv class a little over a month ago, back when Dad was still living on his own. Now, I wonder if I'll even be able to attend the six-week series that starts tonight, though I'm relieved Lance has shown up to give me a break and let me get back to Charleston for a couple of days. My timing of checking this bucket list item off my list could not be worse.

What the hell was I thinking signing up? I know nothing about improv. What I do know is that I nearly pee my pants laughing every single time I watch a show. I love improv. Is that enough?

I pad through the Theatre 99 lobby, following the voices to the historic auditorium. A handful of people look up at the stage from their bright-red seats. The stage supports a bald man, around my age, smiling broadly through his big beard.

Casual and nonchalant, he sits with his legs dangling off the stage. Solid, cute, bearded, and smiling: just my type. My insta-crush is not helping my stomach, which is already buzzing with nerves. He looks down at me and waves, introducing himself as Josh, our teacher. He must be the teacher. Crap—teacher crushes are the worst.

I wave back and tell him my name.

My fellow students—four women and five men—are scattered all over the theater. We will all take the stage before the night ends, but first, Josh has us stand for some silly icebreaker exercises, which help shake off some of my nerves (likely the point). Still, having come straight from the hospital in my comfy caregiver attire, I am self-conscious.

Josh starts us off with a "cascading" word-association activity, where a one-word cue stimulates our subconscious to connect to other words and ideas. This idea flow will assist us in our improv scenes.

Josh tells us to close our eyes and let our thoughts wander to the first idea that comes to mind from the keyword. Then he shares the word *star*. My mind spins like a compass and lands instantly on the

North Star. I am hit with the image of Dad hanging a North Star in the front yard each Christmas. From there my mind wanders, and I wonder if it was only at Christmastime or if maybe he actually left the star up all year long, which is definitely something Dad would do …

While my mind navigates the spiderweb of neural connections, Josh circles the auditorium, asking each of us to share what associations the word *star* prompt for us. As my turn comes, I panic. The last thing I want to discuss is Dad. My Dad feelings are far too raw and near the surface. In my vulnerable state, I am so worried I'll get upset and deliver the wrong kind of scene during my very first improv class.

I try to pursue another association with star, *any other* association. I am desperately seeking a connection that doesn't involve Dad, but that damn compass won't budge from the North Star. I can find no alternative word or thought. My inner monologue is, *Star, star, star … think, think, think … Jaclyn!* while everyone else gracefully shares their stars.

The woman in front of me with long, dark, curly hair is talking about a famous Hollywood star. *Shit, I'm next. Shit!*

Josh calls my name and asks me to share what *star* makes me think of. I sit quietly for a beat, and the curly-haired lady offers me a sweet, encouraging smile. Awkwardly, I share with Josh and the class how the word reminds me of the North Star that hung in my parents' yard for many years.

I hope Josh will leave it at that. But he kindly presses further, saying, "And then what do you think of from there?"

Shit! Why does he have to be such a good teacher?

This is what I'd feared. Unable to think my way out of the trap, I blurt out, "I just wonder where the star is now, which worries me because I need to find it because my dad is in the hospital and has lost his mind and everything is all fucked up, and I have no idea what's going to happen to his house or to him or his cat, and I just need to find that star before it's too late!"

Mortified by my verbal diarrhea, I look at Josh apologetically. He smiles tenderly and nods. "You'll find it," he gently offers as he looks straight into my eyes.

Josh then releases me from his gaze and moves right along to the next student, as if my outburst was no big deal. The way he handled it leaves me feeling instantly safe and assured. I know I belong.

JANUARY 25, 2022

"Just do exactly what I tell you to do, Jaclyn," Dad says from his bed as he guides me into the perfect golf stance. I follow his instructions, hoping nobody walks by his room to see me swinging a pretend golf club.

"When your hips are open like that, it allows the swing to happen naturally. See? That's perfect!" Dad proclaims. I smile and nod at him, thanking him for the golf lesson. Dad has been a golf-teaching professional for the last thirty years, and I know he must be missing it.

Over the past seven years as a widower, Dad has experienced many health issues. His ailments certainly haven't aided his golf game or instruction. Before his ambulance ride to this hospital, Dad suffered from diabetes, heart disease, and kidney failure. All these issues left lingering blood clots in his legs, created major swelling, and forced him to provide golf lessons while seated in a chair.

No golf-pro myself, I thought it sounded crazy. Who in their right mind would want to take golf lessons from an old guy who could barely stand? I was pleasantly surprised to learn that I was wrong, and Dad is such a talented golf instructor that his clients were honored to have his attention, even if he instructed them from a seated position.

After freely receiving this valuable lesson that many others had paid for, I walk back to "my" chair, the one I've occupied for most of the last three weeks. Dad's eyes quickly widen. "What are you doing?" he asks.

I reach for my laptop to get some work done. I work in human resources for a publishing company in Charleston, and they are amazingly kind to me as I navigate this difficult situation. They allow me to work from Dad's hospital room, though I try to return to Charleston once a week for improv class and to work from our office for a day or so. The fact that my company cares about me and I don't have to fear for my job is the biggest blessing.

"I'm not done with your lesson," Dad says curtly, giving me a hard look and waiting for me to stand back up.

We have been at it with this lesson for more than thirty minutes, and I can't take it anymore. Also, I have a project to do for my boss, Ben, that I need to complete by the end of the day.

"I'm sorry, Dad. I have some work I really need to do. Let's pick the lesson back up later," I say casually, opening my laptop.

I feel Dad's eyes boring into me from across the room, and I look up just as he screams, "God dammit, Jaclyn, you are so goddamn defiant. You've always been defiant. You don't give a shit about what anyone else wants or needs. Why are you even here?"

I stare at Dad, feeling as though he's just slapped me square across my jaw. I open my mouth to speak, but nothing comes out. What can I possibly say to him?

The only defiance I've ever expressed was in refusing to magically become a writer. Otherwise, I've always been the most compliant of children. For forty-three years, I've consistently done nearly everything he's asked of me or told me to do. My compliance is half an act of love in an attempt to win his approval and half an act of fear trying to not upset him. The end result has left me one of the most people-pleasing humans on the planet, hardly defiant.

The Dad I know and love might lose his temper, but he would never speak to me like that. He would never assassinate my character. I understand that he is confused and has no idea who he is or where he is at any given moment. Though the hospital staff instructed me to go along with his delusions, to not cause confusion, that was easy for them to say; they never knew any other version of my dad.

This moment, it is just too much. I swallow my sorrows and look at Dad. I apologize as I place my laptop in my backpack. With tears prickling my eyes, I tell Dad I am going to the cafeteria to grab lunch and get some work done. When I ask if he wants me to bring him back anything, he just scoffs at me like I am some sort of golf washout, a defiant quitter.

I walk down the long hallways of the hospital, step into the elevator, and actively avoid eye contact with anyone. I'm usually a very friendly person, but I have nothing to say to anyone. I grab a premade turkey sandwich and Diet Coke. At the cash register, I share a smile with the kind woman who has sold me sandwiches nearly every day for the past few weeks. *God, does she ever get a day off?* I take my cellophane-wrapped lunch to a small table as far away from the hustle and bustle as I can get on the edges of the noisy cafeteria.

Work has piled up, but I also have messages about Dad and coworkers asking how I am holding up. Overwhelmed by my luck at being part of such a supportive work environment, I take a few mindful moments to respond to each message. Once caught up, I open a browser tab to google the term *advanced vascular dementia*, a phrase that doctors keep throwing around to see if it sticks as Dad's official diagnosis.

From the Johns Hopkins website, I read, "Vascular dementia is the second most common form of dementia, after Alzheimer's disease," and, "It's caused when decreased blood flow damages the blood tissue."[1] I can't find anything unique by adding *advanced* to the term, so I guess *advanced* is just an adjective meaning really freaking bad.

How could this have happened overnight? Dad was certainly never "normal," but when did he cross over from quirkily eccentric to clinically demented? Yes, his forgetfulness and oddness had increased with age, but damn, now we have Tom Brady in a spaceship and hospital golf lessons. It seems to have come out of absolutely nowhere.

If Dad did not have a recent stroke, what caused his extremely decreased blood flow? Are they just giving up because they can't find what is actually wrong with him? Why is aging such a mystery when so many people do it?

Sitting in the cafeteria, I feel my phone vibrate in my pocket and look down to see a text message from one of my best friends, Corinne, asking how I am doing and for an update on Dad's condition. God, I love that woman. We've been friends for so long, she may as well be my sister. I am comforted to hear from her right when I need her the most, even though she is hundreds of miles away.

I smile and think about my four best friends. We call ourselves the McGee family, an inside joke. Three of them have been in my life since I was a kid. They are always with me in spirit, but I so wish any one of them was there with me in the cafeteria. If I'm being honest, I really wish I had a husband with me with a large manly shoulder to

---

1   Johns Hopkins Medicine, "Dementia," n.d., https://www.hopkinsmedicine.org/health/conditions-and-diseases/dementia#:~:text=Vascular%20dementia%20(VaD)%20is%20the,root%20causes%20of%20these%20conditions.

cry on. I want that man who would look tenderly at me and say, "It's OK, baby, I got you. I'm here."

That is a joke, such an idea! I've been dealing with parental health problems for the past decade and never had a man to offer support. Hell, I haven't even had a serious relationship in a decade! I can't even remember what a large manly shoulder feels like. My girl squad, the sisters McGee, have supported me through everything else in my life, and they will get me through this too. I learned long ago that real life isn't a romantic comedy; it's a tragic one.

FEBRUARY 9, 2022

More than a month's worth of mail spills across the foyer floor, forming drifts against random objects like golf clubs, a walker, and a stack of twenty-year-old *Cat Fancy* magazines. I step around the piles for the moment and drag a hard wooden chair from the kitchen into the foyer. In Dad's kitchen, it has served as his impromptu work chair, pulled up to the impromptu desk he carved out of the kitchen island. Of course, Dad has an actual desk elsewhere in the house, but Desk 1.0 is unusable, buried beneath geological layers of paper. Dad's kitchen island became Desk 2.0, until it, too, was overcome by his mess.

So, there I sit, in the middle of Dad's foyer using my lap as Desk 3.0. The foyer is the closest I can get to the front door, and when the stench of cat urine overwhelms me, I can open the door and snag a few drags of fresh air. Dad surrendered the fight against cat-urine stench many years ago. He'd been surrendering battle after battle since Mom died. And as much as I hate to admit it, it seems unlikely Dad will ever return to this home again. Such a painful thought, I try to avoid it like a sharp object.

I compartmentalize and focus on this one task to preserve what sanity I have left. *One problem at a time, Jaclyn.* The problem du jour is those drifts of bills. I give myself pep talks. I dig through endless piles of mail with the one goal of collecting the most recent bill from each utility company or bill collector.

As if I am engaged in an Easter egg hunt or bizarro bingo game, I celebrate each time I locate the most recent electricity, water, and cable bill. I don't even bother opening them yet—it is enough that I found them. I will go through them at the hospital the following day. My process is working for me until ... I discover Dad's American Express bill.

Good God! It's almost twenty thousand dollars! My memory of Dad putting Mom's funeral expenses on this card seven years ago comes to mind. He put the entire expense on one credit card. Watching the funeral home woman swipe that card made me feel nauseated, knowing Dad would spend the rest of his life paying for his wife's funeral expenses. Now, here in their foyer in a home they no longer occupy is the proof.

Then I find Dad's Medicare statement and have almost finished this terrible task when I find the envelope from Dad's reverse mortgage company. Across the front in big bold letters, it reads, "Final Notice." I open the envelope like I am defusing a bomb.

Dad is several months behind on his reverse mortgage insurance payments, and unless a large payment is made soon, he will be in breach of his contract. He is close to losing the house. Sitting in the foyer that day, I can't even remember how long it has been since Mom and Dad chose a reverse mortgage. Even then I didn't think it was a good idea, but what the hell did I know? I was young and had no idea how mortgages worked, but they did and should have known better.

What I did know was that Dad took a lump payment from the reverse mortgage in the beginning. He received hundreds of thousands of dollars and would not have to pay a mortgage after that. However, a reverse mortgage had a price. He was to remain in the house until the bitter end. Bitterly, I now realize that the end is in sight.

If he were in his right mind, he could sell the house and repay the lump sum and all the accrued interest. However, he is not in his right mind or physically up to the task. Dad's house is a complete wreck.

In addition to allowing the house to take on the perpetual stench of cat piss, Dad is a hoarder. It is a problem that has worsened in step with the loss of Mom and his declining health. I don't think the house has even been cleaned at all in the past four years, not since I gave up attempting to help Dad clean the house. On two separate occasions, I took time off work to try to "de-hoard" the house just so it could then be properly cleaned. In desperation, I even hired help with this monumental task.

Dad agreed to the whole thing ahead of time, but as soon as we started clearing a path, it was over. Everything I dragged out of the garage or the house, from old, cracked windows that could never be used again to dead Christmas lights, returned like a bad penny. Dad undermined all my efforts to help, angrily dragging his broken treasures off the curb and back up the drive to the house. After a few hours of this weird passive-aggressive game of fetch, I forfeited the match.

Dad and Mom had many cats over the years, sometimes as many as six at one time. The cats established the habit of peeing wherever and whenever they pleased. Finally, down to just one living cat, a feral rescue named Colby, the smell of his predecessors has outlived them all. If cats have nine lives, their urine must have ninety.

Dad had accepted that I refused to stay over with the house in that condition and didn't balk when I told him I'd be staying at a nearby hotel. The hotel was lonely and made my visits melancholic. I longed for a more traditional setup. I entertained visions of fun father-daughter cookouts and watching movies in the living room.

That never happened. I could never eat at Dad's house because the plates were filthy and for fear of bug infestations or spoilage.

That day in the foyer, I look at the reverse mortgage insurance statement again, unsure how to process it. Part of me is naturally concerned with the threat, but the other part shrugs it off. The house is likely a moot point.

Absent a miraculous and rapid recovery, Dad will probably be discharged into a nursing home from the hospital. I've been forced to process so much disorienting information over the past month that I need to pace myself. So I take a deep breath, collect the small pile of bills that I need to pay, and say goodbye to Colby before I walk out the front door.

FEBRUARY 25, 2022

Aided by Gary, his physical therapist, Dad takes a few steps from his hospital bed to the chair. Gary is the only physical therapist Dad will work with, and I believe it is because he is male. Despite playing Barbies and My Little Pony with me when I was little, when it comes to being supported in a hospital gown barely covering his ass, Dad feels more comfortable with fellow naval veteran Gary. It is Gary who finally gets Dad out of his hospital bed to walk for the first time in nearly two full months.

The hospital staff is pleased to see Dad able to get out of bed and walk, but he is still very confused and agitated most of the time. He is frequently unaware of his surroundings and can't remember why he is there. Time and time again, Dad will look at me and tell me he needs to go to the back of the house to lie down. Then he points behind him like he is at home and wants to go to his bedroom. Other times, he'll ask me to please help him to the kitchen. These requests grow so frequent that I stop being surprised by his surprise.

Lance joins me on the day we choose to tell Dad the truth, that he is never going to be able to return home and that he is going to a veteran's nursing home. Finding a space for him in one of the few homes in South Carolina comes down to whichever one has a bed available.

How is someone supposed to tell their father that he can never go home? Lance isn't the emotional type, so I pin my hopes on his taking the reins to deliver this information to Dad in a way that he can both understand and handle emotionally.

Lance and I both spoke to attorneys for advice on how to proceed with Dad's home and his finances. Unfortunately, things have gone too far, and it is no longer possible for either of us to obtain power of attorney from Dad. Instead, all we can do is seek guardianship through the court system. Even that will not empower us to handle Dad's finances on his behalf.

Conservatorship is a better option to enable us to help Dad, but that will take several months and cost thousands of dollars. Lance and I have not come to a full decision. However, we are both leaning toward letting the reverse mortgage company foreclose on the house and take it.

The cost of wrangling control to list it, much less restoring it to a state where anyone would even *consider* buying it, might cost us money we don't have. While the realtor I brought on for a walk-through was polite enough to pretend that she saw potential, you simply can't "visualize" away the stench of cat piss. Her estimate of the value of the home was the most telling: it was so dismal that it only bolstered our opinion that the reverse mortgage company deserved the house.

And then there was the cat. Colby, poor Colby. Through research, I located the cat rescue Colby came from. When I notified them of Dad's condition and poor prognosis, they graciously agreed to rehome Colby. Rehoming pets is such a fraught decision. It's far too easy when life is stable to assume you will never, ever leave a beloved pet to the whims of the universe.

In a perfect world, I would have taken Colby home to Charleston. Sadly, as a feral rescue, Colby had a lot of socialization problems. He didn't trust anyone, barely even Dad. Of course, Colby wasn't litter-box trained, and with my own two cats, I would have found myself firmly rooted in crazy cat lady territory. I couldn't bear the thought of my lovely little home smelling like Dad's dilapidated house. Bringing Colby home wouldn't have been fair to Colby, me, or my existing pets.

When the lady from the cat rescue cornered Colby with a net trap, the image of this terrified, confused cat being removed from the only home he'd ever known was awful. All the more so for how much he resembled his terrified, confused former owner who was also removed from his home. Surrendering a pet is not a moral failing; it's the hardest thing many people will ever have to do during one of the hardest moments of their entire lives.

With these difficult choices made, it is now time to tell Dad what is happening. I look at Lance with pleading eyes that beg, "Please do it; I can't do it. Please be the grown-up in the room today."

Lance asks Dad if he understands why he is in the hospital. Confused, Dad looks at each of us, one at a time, before hazarding a guess: "I know I'm confused, and I'm not getting better."

We nod, then Lance tells Dad the whole story of how he got there, even though we both told him this same story several times.

Starting from when he was found unconscious at home, Lance then explains Dad's medical prognosis and moves on to Dad's house. As tactfully as he can, Lance explains that Dad never gave either of us power of attorney to handle his affairs, and that has left us few options. Lance explains to Dad that his doctors don't think it's safe for him to go home again.

Then comes the hard sell: we have to send Dad to live in a "really nice facility with other veterans." God, I hope it's nice and not a shithole, though I suppose he won't remember that we sold it as nice.

Lance assures Dad that he doesn't have to worry about anything anymore because the VA and Medicare will help cover most of the cost. Lance does a great job as a spin doctor, like this terrible situation is really a means for a better future for Dad. At the veteran's home, he'll be carefree and have such a nice, peaceful life.

The spin may have worked better than we expected, or maybe in that moment Dad just gives up on everything like he gave up cleaning and caring for his home years ago. Dad simply nods and says he understands the situation. The look in his eyes indicates that he is still confused but understood enough. It is clear he has no fight left in him. If surrendering Colby was hard, watching my dad surrender the remains of his independence is one of the most heartbreaking moments of my life.

I reach over and hug Dad tightly, promising him that everything is going to be OK. I keep saying and promising things I don't believe. I meant what I said when I told him I would make sure he was taken care of and that I'd visit him all the time. Dad just keeps nodding, looking more tired with every word I say to him.

Finally, after all the hard things have been said, the one unspoken hard thought that remains lodged in the back of my mind is a question:

Am I a terrible, heartless daughter for not taking my dad into my own home and sending him to a nursing home?

TRUST YOUR SCENE PARTNERS

Trust that your scene partner has your back and is committed to creating something great together. Trusting your partner allows you to take creative risks and explore new ideas without fear of judgment or rejection.

Lance's biological father died young from an aggressive form of cancer, leaving behind a young widow and their three-year-old son. After some years of hardship and barely making ends meet, things changed for the pair in December 1972 when Shelby Smith laid eyes on Mom for the first time at a Christmas party. The way Dad retold it, with great zest and frequency, was, "Your mother was wearing white hot pants and white go-go boots and was the most beautiful woman I had ever seen."

Mom didn't rush to a second marriage, but one year in, Dad moved in with her and Lance, and they settled into life before making it official. Dad popped the big question to Mom, and on January 29,

1977, they were married in a little church in Arlington, Virginia, surrounded by family.

Lance stood up at the altar with Mom and Dad, dressed in a navy suit with a red tie and a big white corsage. Mom was beautiful, of course, in a white dress that looked like it was made for her even though she'd bought it right off the rack in a DC department store. Dad wore a gray suit, gray tie, and a twin corsage to Lance's, though it didn't look quite as big on the grown man. With that ceremony, they made the marriage legal, and their family was blended.

Dad was a bit of a *good-time guy* when he met my mom. He drank too much and smoked a pack a day. Mom and Lance both had a calming effect on him. He finally quit smoking a few years after moving in with them, simply because Lance asked him to after he learned about the dangers of smoking at school and brought home visual aids from elementary school.

Just like that, Dad quit, cold turkey. Maybe it was the compelling arguments of an eight-year-old boy. Maybe it was the fact that this child who had already lost one father loved Dad enough to put in the effort and ask him to stop smoking. Either way, Dad was moved to quit, and he never picked up another cigarette.

The love was real, but the dynamics were complicated. Dad and Lance didn't have an easy relationship. If I'm being fair, very few people had an *easy* relationship with our dad.

Dad seemed to travel through life dropping eggshells wherever he went, and the rest of us walked accordingly. Even with the very best intentions, all the love in the world, and under the best of circumstances, a blended family requires an intentional transition. Dad joining their family brought inevitable growing pains.

Dad played his part, and he and Mom attended Lance's games and tournaments. Mom was den mother for Lance's Cub Scout group for several years, a privilege made possible by having a second income. Life was good, mostly better. Though, according to family folklore, Dad and Lance argued often. As the years passed, Dad continued to lose battles in his personal war to not become his own volatile father. Unfortunately, there was always collateral damage, and Lance took the brunt of it.

Mom's lifestyle and financial struggles were bettered by their marriage. She no longer carried the weight of sole responsibility as a single mom in the early 1970s, but the trade-off for her security was the tension between Lance and Dad. Dad's frequent temper flares were usually directed at Lance. It must have been hard for the little boy to accept that, after his biological dad was gone, he had to share his mom with this new man. Whether he liked it or not, with no choice or say in the matter, Lance had a new dad and authority figure who didn't give the little boy much time or space to adapt. Mom always played the role of peacemaker, trying to calm Dad and get him to back off of Lance.

When Dad kept his temper in check, they were happy. Shortly after they married, Mom became pregnant, and they decided to move their growing little family from DC to Richmond, Virginia, a more family-friendly town. With a new two-story home in the suburbs, a wonderful son, and a baby on the way, they both had everything they'd always wanted. The house-proud little family added another new addition, an orange cat named Brandy, who initiated a streak of ginger cats in the Smith family homes.

But domestic bliss was primed for a lightning strike. Shortly after becoming pregnant, Mom was diagnosed with cervical cancer. This life-threatening complication meant that she was now facing an extremely high-risk pregnancy. Her obstetrician told her she should terminate and begin cancer treatment. Continuing to term was medically inadvisable, and having this baby was dangerous for her. She could lose her life if they proceeded with the pregnancy.

Mom and Dad could not accept this advice and were determined to find a doctor who would support the pregnancy and the birth. They sought out two more doctors until they found one, Dr. Dunn, who agreed to treat mom's cancer *and* support her through the pregnancy and birth. Spoiler alert: Dr. Dunn delivered yours truly several months later.

Lance was twelve when I came along, and, from what I've heard, I was a handful. Apparently, I sucked up all the attention in every room I was in like a cherubic energy vampire. I was Mommy's little miracle, a cancer-beating baby. I was Daddy's little girl and his first and only biological child. All this surely contributed to my being somewhat spoiled. Even if he denied it, I could never blame Lance if, as I suspect, he resented and, at times, disliked me a little.

You can't win 'em all. For my part, I adored Lance and sought out his company and approval.

But Lance loved video games, and I loved Lance. Always wanting to be near him, I was thrilled when he taught me how to play *Frogger* on his Atari. But I had my limits. Lance was into Dungeons & Dragons and *Star Trek*, neither of which I would ever learn to appreciate.

Occasionally forced to babysit me, Lance hated this unpaid labor. However, babysitting gave him an opportunity to torment me and lock me in my room until just before our parents came home. Like all older siblings, Lance blamed things on me. He gave me full credit for breaking a lamp in the living room that was actually the victim of his forbidden indoor soccer antics. When he blamed it on me, I was dumb enough to take the fall without protesting. All's fair in sibling rivalry: it was all payback for me being a bratty little sister who always got her way.

Instinctually, I knew I wouldn't get in as much trouble for the broken lamp. I had the social capital that comes from being the youngest child and only girl. We all knew where we stood on the eggshell continuum that set off Dad's temper, and I knew Lance did not have the same buffer. Perhaps I accepted the blame as a subconscious act of kindness, or maybe I just wanted my brother's approval as much as I wanted Dad's.

Lance dreamed of being a pilot in the air force, and right after high school graduation, he enlisted, packed up his things, and headed out to basic. He rarely returned to visit after he left home. I was only six years old when he joined the armed forces, and my remaining childhood years would be spent as an only child in our house.

I always wished for more siblings. I treasured time spent at friends' homes observing their interactions with siblings and entertained by their noisy lives. Their homes were much more boisterous and fun than my quiet home where the joyful noise of children could not be generated by one child … one hand clapping and all that.

. . .

Mom really dug into her feminine side as a wife and mom to a young girl. She had great raw material—runway-model tall with perfect curves and shiny blond hair. Her skin was flawless, a creamy tan, and silky to the touch, and she mastered the art of exactly-right makeup … never too much, never too little. She never left the house without lipstick.

Growing up, I envied my mother's style and fashion sense. Perhaps my fashion aspirations as a Hello Kitty button designer were subconsciously my attempt to make her proud. Each weekend, Mom and I would dress for a Saturday afternoon shopathon (there was so much shopping). At the dawn of the 1990s, my mom was right on trend, pulled together in her perfectly cut jeans, trendy silk vest with a matching silk blouse underneath. Only my mom could level up a vest like that. She finished off the look with stylish flats and matching accessories. It was effortless, and even now I still hope that one day I will be as classy and as fashionable as she was. Was that even possible?

One of her favorite things, outside of shopping, was to hide behind a door in a hallway and jump out and scare me. She'd laugh and laugh and laugh like a little kid. I took it like a good sport in the moment, but then I stalked off vowing to never let her get me like that again. In so many of our family photos, Mom's mouth is spread wide open with laughter. As much as she loved playing jokes, Mom could take them just as well. A witty quip or a funny comeback was always at the ready. Even if I didn't get her fashion sense, she certainly passed her humor on to me.

Mom adored music as much as she loved laughter. Her favorite band was the Rolling Stones, but honorable mentions went to Elton John, Rod Stewart, and the Beatles. Fun fact: on February 11, 1964, my mom was at the first ever Beatles concert in America, at Washington Coliseum. That was two days after their first appearance on the *Ed Sullivan Show*.

I'm fairly certain my mom was the only one in my neighborhood who saw concert footage on MTV and could honestly say, "I was there." I had the coolest mom, but she was also so strong.

Mom rose to any occasion with grace. While she was still hospitalized after a terrible car accident as a teenager, her dad died suddenly. Back home, her own mom was a new mother to her much younger baby brother, George. Within a few years, as a new mother herself, Mom was suddenly watching her seemingly healthy young husband succumb to cancer. All this long before she beat her own cancer diagnosis during her pregnancy with me.

If anyone could have handled this situation with Dad in the hospital and losing his home, it would have been Mom. If anyone could understand how hard it is for me to show up with a smile on these dark days, it would be Mom. But Mom had been dead for seven years, and her absence in Dad's last year feels as profound and daunting as it did when I lost her the first time.

• • •

Dad's mother died from cancer when I was baby after she survived a lifetime of her husband's alcoholism and violent temper. Dad was often pulled into the middle of their arguments. When his father lost control, Dad had to involve the neighbors or even call the police for help. Imprinted by these dynamics, one of Dad's greatest inner conflicts was the fear that he inherited his father's temper.

Dad was the oldest. His younger brothers were twins, Frank and Ronnie, who shared that mysterious and exclusive bond known only to twins. Dad always felt like the outsider, unable to truly penetrate the strong twin bond, though just as he continued boosting my writing career, he never gave up.

• • •

Dad set an example by volunteering in the community. He didn't just show up, he actively sought ways to volunteer, and I was always included in his searches and activities.

Despite having a short temper, Dad had the biggest heart. He genuinely wanted to help others. Dad wanted to make the world a better place. He didn't push me like he did with writing; he set the example.

The results were immediate; we collected food for the less fortunate when I was small, and I volunteered at a cat shelter as a teen. Over the years, many cats came home with me from this shelter, and in turn my parents became serious cat lovers, especially Mom. The results were lasting, as my charitable impulses have only sharpened with age.

• • •

Before the sleep of the dead that accompanies adolescence took its hold on me, at the onset of each spring, Dad would wake me up at the ungodly hour of 6:00 a.m. on Saturday mornings. Excitedly he would burst into my room and announce it was time to go "look for signs of spring." Coffee in one hand, my little fingers in the other, Dad led me down our street to the lake near our home.

In the morning hush, Dad and I walked through the remnants of brown leaves left threadbare by the ravages of winter. Dad made a sort of I-Spy adventure, pointing out the smallest glimmers of nature's beauty emerging in this muddy in-between. So many little things that I didn't even notice, that I would never have noticed, were his priceless talismans—his Signs of Spring.

Dad would bend down and gently hold a newly bloomed white dogwood flower in his hand and say, "See, Jaclyn, here is a sign of spring." Tired and disoriented as I was, I looked into my dad's face, full of joy and hope, and I would quietly nod in awe, not at the flower but at what the flower brought out in my father.

We'd walk a few paces before he would stop to point out the bluebell flowers starting to bud. Their brown leaves long out of season, discarded and forgotten, the trees showed off their plush green finery the way I showed off my pastel Easter dresses. The spring air smelled uniquely clean and light.

The Signs of Spring walk lasted about an hour and became an annual tradition for Dad and me, and it made Dad so happy. It made me happy, too, mostly because it made him so happy.

. . .

Dad was decades ahead of his time as an involved father. He often played Barbies with me and would laugh and smile as we changed the Barbies' outfits over and over again, matching our dolls using different accessories. We also played My Little Ponies and would make believe that our ponies were on a fabulous pony ranch, and then we'd tuck them into their stable for the night at bedtime.

Dad watched over me as I rode my bike in our cul-de-sac with the neighborhood boys. He taught me how to jump off the high dive at the neighborhood pool, even though I was afraid to do so. Always persistent, Dad took weeks and weeks to convince me to do it, and he won me over. He went to the effort of finding father-daughter dances, before the internet, and then proudly escorted me to every single one he found. He always presented me with a beautiful flower corsage for my wrist before each dance.

Dad was just as comfortable in the kitchen as Mom was. They would tag team roasting turkeys, making bread stuffing, and whipping up countless wonderful sides. To this day, Thanksgiving is my favorite holiday, and I think it came from my dad loving it so much.

Even as a little girl, I understood my dad was more sensitive than most men. None of the other men I knew—my uncles, my friends' fathers, my uncle George, and my brother, Lance—were as sensitive as Dad. As the years went on, I would see this more and more clearly.

Dad loved to write. Whether that meant writing a letter for the adult me when I was still just a baby or picking up twenty-five postcards for family and friends while on every single vacation, he was an expressive man. Dad also loved to read, and both my parents spent hours reading to me every night.

As dreamy and nearly ideal as my childhood was, Dad did have a dark side to him. I suppose you can't grow up in such a chaotic home and come out of it undamaged. His anger issues meant he would lose his temper very easily. Ironically, he tried to cope by controlling everything and everyone else, until something went wrong. Then he lost all control. When I spilled some milk at the dinner table as a young kid, Dad completely lost his mind over it, yelling and screaming like I'd committed a murder.

Mom grabbed paper towels quickly and helped me clean it up. She tried to calm him down. She was always trying to calm him down. I learned from her, and I worked overtime as a child to try not to awaken the Mr. Hyde that lurked inside my dad.

The unpredictable eruptions informed my ever-growing anxiety. In the aftermath of each explosion, I took note to never ever do again whatever I had done to drive that look on my dad's face. I'd spend hours in my bedroom, in silent repentance and devastation that I couldn't be a more perfect child for my dad. The problem with control freaks is that they convert everyone around them to perfectionists in the hope that perfection will keep them calm.

As a young and effectively only child, I was more than a little obsessed with my parents. I didn't know whether or not my attachment was unhealthy; it was just how it was. When they would go out for an evening on the town and hire a babysitter, I didn't feel like I was getting a night off.

Instead, I spent the time crying and ruminating about all the things that could happen to them while they were out of my sight. What if they were in a car accident? What if they were kidnapped or murdered? Every ridiculous scenario would run through my little brain until I had to rush to the bathroom to vomit. Even before things escalated, I was an anxious kid.

• • •

When I was a kid, Dad took a position in the paper business for a company called Reynold's. He was a businessman, and I didn't really know what that meant (still don't). He once told me he helped with office efficiency, which definitely sounds like him. I just knew that Dad was gone most Monday through Thursday nights and back home on Fridays. When he was in town during the week, we didn't see him a whole lot because he was working. He and I were both aware of the distance it put between us.

On a Wednesday night when I was nine years old, Mom and I were on our own again since Dad had to travel. We had a frozen dinner that evening, and I spent about an hour afterward outside in the backyard, chasing fireflies.

Around 9:00 p.m. I had just taken a bath in my own bathroom at the top of the stairs. Mom was lying on her bed, talking on the phone with Dad. They talked every night when he traveled.

Wrapped in a faded burgundy towel, I stepped into the hallway to see a man running out the front door. The entire scene was like a dream. I wandered into my parents' bedroom and said, "Mom, who was that running out the front door?" She looked at me like I had announced a spaceship on the lawn.

Mom told Dad to hold on a moment, and she put the phone down on the bed. She slowly walked out of the bedroom and into the hallway and glanced down the stairway. Her eyes zeroed in on the key to the dead bolt, its ring swinging with the force of a recently slammed door.

She raced back to the phone and confirmed that someone had indeed just left our home. Details of what happened next have drained away like my bathwater from that night, but I do remember the police coming and searching our home. They found that nothing had been taken.

The police speculated that the perpetrator was startled when he saw me and fled. They never figured out who it was or why he had entered our house in the first place. Dad didn't care about who or why; he just cared that it had happened at all. He was devastated by the fact that his wife and daughter had been in danger and he hadn't been there to protect them.

Dad came home immediately, and the next week he told his boss he would no longer be able to travel for work. Dad was transferred to a new position to ensure no travel. His new position was located just outside Atlanta, Georgia, in a town called Marietta.

EMBRACE FAILURE AND BE ADAPTABLE

In improv, not every choice will land perfectly, and that's OK. Embracing failure means being willing to take risks, knowing that some characters may not work out as planned. Improv scenes are constantly evolving, and you must be adaptable to change.

APRIL 4, 2022

The past few months have been a sweet-and-sour parfait, layered with horrifyingly sad moments and topped with soft, beautiful ones that enveloped me like a little hug, exactly when I needed one. Call it serendipity or synchronicity, but it's no simple coincidence that the day I am moving Dad into the Veterans' Victory House (VVH) in Walterboro, South Carolina, is also the day I start my level 2 improv class at Theatre 99.

I'm not sure I would have survived these months without improv. Anchored in Myrtle Beach four to six days a week, I've forced myself to drive back to Charleston each Sunday for my improv class. The class and the detoxifying drive away from the dying place containing what remains of my father, my childhood, my family … it is respite. Improv forces me to breathe fresh air after drowning in the stagnancy of a hospital with Dad.

In improv class I can let everything go … every little awful thing that is happening in that hospital with Dad. Improv class is a black box blocking out anything other than improv. Just as boundaries enable a small child to thrive, improv keeps my mind from wandering into the dangerous wilderness of fear and loss. Forced to live in the moment surrounded by other people with no intention other than to have fun, I love the moment, and the moment loves me back.

I'm certain that counterbalance gets me through the day I put Dad in "the home." I count my blessings. In addition to improv, I am also blessed by an incredible boss who let me take yet another day off to do this ugly thing. It is never lost on me how fortunate I am to work for a company that supports all aspects of life.

Standing in the VVH parking lot, leaning on my car, I freeze as the paramedics from Myrtle Beach open the back doors of the ambulance, lift the stretcher out, and place it onto pavement. Dad, my daddy, is lying on the stretcher, screaming at the top of his lungs, and crying like a child. My heart all but collapses in the few steps it takes me to rush to the stretcher.

"Is he in pain?" I ask quietly.

"No," replies the EMT, "he's just very confused and in a highly agitated state. We've given him a sedative to try to calm him down." This paramedic tries to comfort me because he cannot comfort Dad.

I rest my hand on Dad's forearm and tell him the softest lie: "Everything is going to be OK." Even as my words mix with the tears running into Dad's ears, I chastise myself. How many times have I said that lie the past few months?

EMBRACE FAILURE AND BE ADAPTABLE

Then I equivocate, attempt to soothe myself because no one else is left to soothe me. Maybe it's not a lie; maybe somehow everything will be OK one day. Maybe I am lying to Dad but not to myself. I don't know the truth from a lie, wishful thinking from hope. I just know Dad is lying in the parking lot of a building constructed to honor brave military veterans, crying and feeling just as alone as I do.

Taking no comfort in my hollow words, he screams, "Get me out of here!" And then, "Someone help me" as the paramedics open the double doors of the VVH and roll his stretcher inside. I follow right behind them, in a state of shock that this is all truly happening, that this is real.

"God, please take me now, take me now!" he cries in the parking lot, through the double doors, and again as the paramedic attempts to stop Dad's stretcher by the front desk long enough to complete the intake paperwork.

Dad continues pleading to the Lord above to take him while I try to focus on paperwork, my eyes darting all around until I notice a pungent smell in the air, which seems to be coming from Dad. To be fair, I can't be sure it's Dad, as this place has its own brew of odd and unsettling odors. I look away from the paperwork, first at Dad, and then beseechingly at the paramedic closest to him.

Unlike me, this paramedic has seen it all. He whispers to me, "I believe he's defecated himself, ma'am ... we're going to go ahead and get him to his room to get him cleaned up and settled."

The woman at the front desk, who has also seen it all and is waiting for her clipboard full of papers that I'm struggling to complete, deftly instructs the paramedic where to take Dad. I watch Dad, screaming and crying, being rolled down the hallway. I'm simultaneously glad to have him and his smell moving away from me and overwhelmed by guilt for taking any relief. The weight of the moment is almost too much for me to bear.

I return to the clipboard, detached as I watch my own hand gripping a pen. I collapse into the first chair I can find in the vestibule of the home. I am in a dream, a nightmare really, and I'm not really here. I try to take a few deep breaths, but it's hard to catch the air, and what I can breathe smells like death and feels like desertion, betrayal, and regret.

I'm drowning in this place, and my chest tightens as I gasp for air. At this precarious moment, I don't wish it all away, don't wish my dad was magically all better, or wish that this really was just a dream. What I wish, what my heart wishes without consulting my mind, is that someone was with me right now, anyone really. I wish someone was here to put their arm around me and hug me tightly. I wish I had someone to take this clipboard of paperwork and fill it out for me, to go check on Dad and make sure he's OK. But there's nobody … nobody but me.

In the depths of this despair, a door bursts open across the hallway from me, and an angelic woman floats toward me with a sympathetic smile on her face. She drifts gracefully into my orbit and introduces herself as Lauren. She's not just somebody; she's somebody I know.

The past few weeks, I've been speaking to Lauren since learning that Dad would be coming here. Lauren is the woman I've been sending paperwork to and the sweet soul who has been trying to put me at ease about this insane situation I find myself in. Lauren, answering my unspoken wish, takes the clipboard from me and helps me out of the chair. She guides me into a more comfortable chair in her cheerful little office.

Lauren's office is the antithesis of the dying place; it is alive with the artwork her children made for her, crowded with joyful photos of

EMBRACE FAILURE AND BE ADAPTABLE

family and friends. As comforting as Lauren's presence is, the cheerfulness of her office feels contradictory to my outlook. I don't belong in a cheerful space because I am utterly broken to see Dad in this state. I'm somewhere between Dad's darkening world and Lauren's cheery outlook. I'm in the liminal space between a normal life and my father's death.

Lauren has arrived just in time to break my fall. Even as I'm precariously close to collapsing into despair, my internal monologue is incredulous. How is it even possible for any daughter to see their dad in that state, to smell him like that, to hear him call to the Lord like Fred Sanford feigning a heart attack? (Note to those too young to remember Redd Foxx: google "Fred Sandford's Funniest Heart Attacks"—you can thank me later.)

There should for sure be laws against this. We are in the South, bless our hearts; where are the etiquette police to keep things right?

Lauren tells me I don't need to complete the paperwork on the clipboard because I already emailed her that information. As I look at her, relief washes over me. Lauren informs me that Dad will be going immediately into the quarantine ward of the VVH for fourteen days. This is standard protocol for all new residents, due to the global pandemic. Timing is everything. After fourteen days in quarantine, Dad will go to a "wonderful room," she tells me, with a roommate, and it will be in the Lyon's Unit.

"I need to mentally prepare you for what the quarantine unit looks like," she says, her tone forewarning it's not going to be pretty. "You will have to wear full protective gear every time you go back to see him, which includes a face mask, thin plastic scrubs that go over your clothing, and net booties."

My inner voice sarcastically interjects, "Wow, that won't be confusing at all to Dad."

Lauren goes on, "Also, you will have to sign yourself into the quarantine unit, which is a special sign in outside the unit, not just the regular sign in at the front of the building. And you'll have to enter into the unit through a full plastic, flame-retardant opening that blocks off the unit."

I nod back at her, while the same inner voice deadpans, "I always wanted to be in *E.T.* I could totally have been Drew Barrymore."

"One more thing for now …" Lauren says as I sit in her happy little office chair. "I need to know if you want to sign a Do Not Resuscitate form for your father."

Barely retaining any new information, I stare blankly. "I don't think so …" I say. "Well, should I? I don't even know?"

Now my inner voice is livid. "Fuck! Why is she asking me this, and why am I the person to make these decisions? Where are the adults?" But no matter how much I resent it, fear it, resist it, I am the adult, and while Lauren has guided me out of the hallway into her office, I am still alone.

I share with Lauren how Dad signed a form for me years ago proclaiming that he wanted all the bells and whistles to preserve his life. Because of what he said when he was lucid, I feel I probably should not support a Do Not Resuscitate form for him when he is lost.

Lauren nods like she understands what I am saying but proceeds to explain that Dad has advanced dementia. Therefore, he is not living the best life, and there is no way he could possibly recover or resume a normal existence. She explains the harshest truths as gently as she can. At some point while Dad is with them, he could go into cardiac arrest or have a stroke, and they would of course try to save his life, but not with heroic measures. Instead, they usually let the hero veterans die as naturally as possible, on their own terms, quietly, peacefully, with dignity. Lauren says that this is what most people want.

EMBRACE FAILURE AND BE ADAPTABLE

For a couple of minutes, I sit quietly with her words, struggling to shift my cloudy mind to think properly. For God's sake, this is so serious, and my mind should be clear for this decision, but clarity is highly elusive in this place where dementia patients go to find dignity while crapping themselves in the hallway and screaming for the Lord to take them home.

Finally, I tell Lauren I want to call Lance and get his opinion on this matter. She nods, and I dial Lance's number with my cell phone.

When Lance answers the phone, I tell him about the decision at hand: to resuscitate or not to resuscitate. I have Lance on speakerphone, and Lauren chimes in with her expert opinion, which Lance agrees with. I thank him for his time and hang up the phone.

I look at the Do Not Resuscitate form sitting on Lauren's desk. I pick up the pen sitting next to it. I check the box saying that I agree to "no resuscitating" if Dad stops breathing for any reason, sign the form, place the pen down, and walk out of the cheery little office under the darkest of clouds.

APRIL 9, 2022

It seems as if the entire town of Surfside Beach has shown up for the estate sale I've pulled together in a desperate attempt to raise some funds for Dad's care (and if I'm honest, for his impending funeral, which I'm trying to pretend won't happen). I can't help but wonder if it's because he was such a beloved member of their community or if it's because they have always dreamed of seeing the inside of Dad's *unusual* house. Dad's yard alone indicated that he was eclectic at best, eccentric at worst, and the kind of man who stimulated significant curiosity from his neighbors over the years.

Lance drove up from Atlanta to assist me in this crazy endeavor. I'm extremely grateful he's here along with one of my best friends. Even though she is suffering through a major cold, Sara drove up from Charleston to help. It means the world to me.

Last week my bestie, Corinne, helped create a digital flyer for the estate sale, and I posted on every Myrtle Beach/Surfside Beach Facebook page I could find. Just last night Lance, Sara, and I put up signs all over Surfside Beach, which Sara graciously printed for me, letting everyone know where and when the estate was and that "all proceeds go to help care for a well-known community golf pro and United States veteran."

Standing in the kitchen filled with memories of Mom and Dad, I'm utterly unprepared for all the emotions churning inside me. Emotions are so inconvenient. The estate sale is just one more thing I need to check off my endless to-do list for Dad. So far, I've been successful at pushing my emotions to the side to get things done. I've got this. I just have to focus, put on my game face, but ... this isn't a game.

As I look around at all the items for sale, I'm overwhelmed with the enormity of losing my family. The kitchen counters are piled high with old kitchen appliances, glasses, coffee mugs, and plates. Strangers are rummaging through the kitchen drawers, still full of silverware, cooking utensils, and potholders because we didn't have enough time to empty them all.

I choke back tears when a woman comes toward me with a plate I had given Dad many years ago. It has big red peppers and big black stripes all over it, and I bought it because Dad loves hot sauce. Wait, no, he *loved* hot sauce. I'm not even sure what tense to use when speaking of Dad.

"How much for this plate?" the woman asks me.

EMBRACE FAILURE AND BE ADAPTABLE

I look at the plate again; Sara has been directing folks to me for prices because she doesn't feel comfortable setting prices on my memories. And this was one of Dad's favorites. I see flashes of the breakfasts he ate off that plate: eggs with hot sauce, bagels and cream cheese, all to be hand-washed off his special plate. I can hear the many happy conversations I had with Dad as he was eating off that plate, joking about his bagel concoctions.

I swallow hard and say, "Two dollars," avoiding eye contact. I don't want the woman to see the tears welling up in my exhausted eyes. I don't want her pity.

"I'll give you fifty cents," she says.

Ouch, guess I don't need to worry about pity from this one. Stunned, I slowly nod and take the woman's change, putting it into the black Adidas belt bag I'm wearing.

Lance is manning the outdoor sales, managing tons of people looking at all Dad's plants, pots, yard art, and more. He's also keeping an eye on the garage, which contains about twenty-five years' worth of items, including the dollhouse that Dad made for me as a child.

I'm conflicted as to whether I should take the dollhouse home with me. The sentimentality is strong, but the dollhouse is huge. And the truth is, I have no daughter to give it to and nothing to do with it. This is how I feel about a majority of the items in Mom and Dad's home—no one to pass them on to, nothing to do with them.

While I know these people are a necessary part of the process, like carrion birds and the circle of life, I kind of hate them. I keep fighting the urge to kick all these strangers out of my parents' home, pack up every single thing, and take it all home with me. But I can't, and I know I can't.

For three months, I spent a majority of each week at the hospital with Dad before stopping by his home on my way back to Charleston.

Three months of walking this sad and silent shell of a house so many times, taking items that I deemed extremely sentimental or important, and loading them into my little Honda Civic. But there's no more room in my guest room. I've run out of space for treasures and am forced to be that woman who sells off the remnants of what once was a family. Whether I like it or not, I need the carrion birds to lighten my load, even as they pick at the bones of my childhood.

Sara knows me so well and can see I'm close to breaking down. I embrace her and wonder what I'd do without her, without all my girls. I think about the weekend we spent in Myrtle Beach a couple of weeks ago, all of us girls together, going through my parents' belongings, throwing away everything that could be thrown away.

They rented a beautiful house on the beach, a few miles away from Dad's house. We gathered at his house during the days, getting it ready for this estate sale. We escaped to the rental house at night—drinking wine, playing games, and laughing. I wonder if I'll ever be able to adequately express my gratitude to them. I wonder if they know that in the wreckage of one dying family, I realized that I am not alone. I still have a family, and they are it. They are everything to me.

I'm approached by a man and a woman, with their young daughter in tow. "How much for the primary bedroom furniture set?" the man asks me.

"Um, I don't know—would you like to just make me an offer?" I say. I'm surprised they want the primary bedroom furniture because it's so old and not in great shape.

"We'll take the bed, nightstands, dresser, and also the hutch in the dining room for eight hundred dollars," the man says.

"OK" is all I say, shocked. Is he being generous or getting one over on me? I'm choosing to believe in generosity. After the pepper-plate lady, I need a little hope in humanity.

EMBRACE FAILURE AND BE ADAPTABLE

The man hands me eight hundred dollars in cash and says they'll get a U-Haul truck and be back. An hour later, the U-Haul family has returned, and I'm checking the hutch to be sure everything is out of it before it's carried away. Lance has just joined me. Lance and I begin to guess how much money we've made so far when the man buying the furniture timidly walks into the dining room.

"We found something while taking apart the bed frame that we think you should know about."

Oh god, I think to myself. What the hell is it? A huge stack of *Playboy* magazines? A loaded gun? A duffel bag full of hundred-dollar bills (you can't blame me for being hopeful on such a bleak day).

I brace myself for what the man is about to say, but I can't truly brace myself hard enough because he then says, "It's a dead animal." He pauses and slowly continues with, "I think it's a kitten."

I feel the blood drain from my face, and all I can say is "Nooooooooooooooooo."

Lance sees immediately that this is one situation I am unable to navigate. He jumps up from the dining room chair and springs into action. I watch as my brother heads down the hallway, toward Dad's bedroom, with the man buying the furniture on his heels, and I'm done. As I'm breathing heavily with my hands on my face, Sara comes to my aid, having just heard the dead kitten conversation.

"Let's step outside for a few minutes and get some air," Sara soothes, putting her arm around my shoulders and walking me toward the front door as if I'm a little kid who biffed it on her bicycle.

Sara guides me down the front steps, which are still littered with at least fifteen planters that haven't been purchased, random Christmas decorations left outdoors perhaps for years, and countless birdhouses. Two plastic chairs are sitting in the driveway; I collapse into one of them, and Sara gently eases herself into the other.

I lean forward, resting my elbows on my knees, return my face to my hands, and begin to cry. I cry for the kitten who died and spent years of its afterlife wedged behind my parents' bed. I cry for Dad, who didn't know he was sleeping above a dead kitten under the bed. He doesn't know that strangers are going through his precious belongings and that I'm desperate to sell his things for pennies on the dollar.

I am desperate not just because I can't store all these mementos from his life but because I literally cannot afford his death. I am selling off all these things he can't take with him in an effort to forestall a tremendous debt to cover the patient portion of his nursing home care fees and all his funeral expenses. I cry for all the belongings inside that house that have meant so much to my family over the years and the fact that I physically can't take it all with me.

I cry because I don't know how I am going to keep my family's memories alive when I can't keep their belongings. I cry because I've been put in this impossible situation, which could have been less painful and less of a burden with proper planning. I cry because Dad didn't care enough … about himself, his kids, his life … I don't know which, but he didn't care enough to put things in order, so now I am mired in the chaos of dismantling his life before he's even taken his last breath. I cry because no matter how stoic, loyal, or funny I try to be, this is just so fucking unfair.

Sara just lets me cry it all out and puts her hand on my back occasionally, telling me I'm a great daughter and I'm doing the best I can with the situation that's been dealt to me. In that moment when I've hit bottom and Sara's caught me on the bounce back up, something catches our eyes.

Up in a tree, I see the handmade signs Dad made a few years ago and strung up in the trees. The signs read, *Defeat ALZ* and *ALZ Awareness*. My sobs are now turning into laughter. How the hell are

EMBRACE FAILURE AND BE ADAPTABLE

we going to get those damn signs down, and how did the man with an ironically similar disease get them up in the trees? Sara starts laughing with me. After washing out the dust of this difficult day with my tears, I realize that as long as I have friends by my side to laugh with me, I may just be all right. Maybe I wasn't lying to Dad when I said, "It's going to be OK."

MAY 14, 2022

I'm back at the VVH to visit with Dad, or whoever this new person is, because this shrunken little stranger sounds and looks nothing like my dad. After dropping fifty pounds since this disastrous year began, he now has no clothes that fit him. I've brought a beautiful assortment of Goodwill attire that I hope he accepts. Aside from dipping into my own ever-diminishing funds, I've also invested all my free time addressing things like clothes for the rapidly shrinking man.

Dad's new vintage wardrobe, including several gently worn shirts donated by a kind friend's husband and several new essentials from Target, is my effort to fill some of his endless needs. He needs so much from me and so much of me. Even if I enjoyed the opportunity to dress my dad like my own personal Ken doll, I simply can't afford to buy him clothes. Even Goodwill gave me sticker shock. Although I found an electric-blue polo in the dingy sea of castaways, the options were unimpressive. I nearly keeled over when the lovely cashier announced my total: $125? One hundred and twenty-five dollars ... at Goodwill. Goodwill. This was well before the inflation of 2023, so what the hell, Goodwill?!

I had to suck it up to find my own goodwill. Let's face it: my purchases were probably the former togs of someone else's dad who shrank into nothing and would probably end up back at Goodwill when Dad no longer had a withering body to dress. Until then, we needed to dress his body.

At home, I laundered and folded every article of clothing, then placed each piece into small piles based on their clothing category. Then, armed with a black Sharpie, I wrote "Shelby Smith" on a large brown bag, the way my dad might have scrawled "Jaclyn" on my school lunch thirty years prior. But I'm not packing nourishment for a child. I'm packing used clothes for my dad, who now has the mind of a child in the body of an elderly man. I'm trying to dress a body slowly fading while fearing a mind that's nearly gone.

I get to the VVH and prepare to play the role of the "good daughter," Little Miss Ray of Fucking Sunshine. I slink down the main hallway, stalling to observe the mannequins in uniform from each branch of the US military, displayed with artifacts, flags, and military awards. I mosey past the community room where veterans (mostly men but a few women) gather to play games, read, and watch movies. Then I pause near the end of the hall to enjoy my favorite part of the VVH, the birdcage.

A few vibrant birds flit in their large cage, a lively kaleidoscope of color and life, preening without a care. Their vivacity briefly breaks through my numbness and strain. Caged as they are, the birds are genuinely cheerful, and it helps. I lean toward the cage and talk to the birds.

I wonder how their lives are at the VVH and what they make of it. I wonder if these are elderly birds, which is why they were chosen to live at a nursing home. These thoughts seem entirely logical in this strange wonderland on the other side of the rabbit hole that is Dad's dementia. These bright birds bring me a shred of joy, which I desperately need, to complete my long march to the Lyon's Unit.

EMBRACE FAILURE AND BE ADAPTABLE

After the birds, there's nothing left that I want to see. I try to avert my eyes from the parade of open doors, but the gravity of the place demands my attention. Instead of birds, I see elderly man after elderly man, sitting on their beds or in their wheelchairs, staring blankly at their televisions. Many watch Western movies, filling the hallways with the sounds of galloping horses over the orchestration of cowboy music. Occasionally, I glimpse the edge of a smile while a stranger watches the movies of his youth, transported to a happier time and place. I wish I could go sit with him. Instead, I go on, to the room of a man who never smiles anymore.

I enter Dad's room timidly. I never know what to expect. My lips bend into an involuntary smile, a glimmer of pride and satisfaction in seeing the patriotic USA decorations I used to decorate Dad's door and personalized bulletin board. I've done my best to personalize his meager real estate in the small room he has to share with a roommate.

Last weekend I hung every card that Dad has received since he first entered the hospital months ago. Today I am adding the cards he's received from friends or family since arriving at the nursing home. Half his cards are from me. On the rare occasions I'm not here with Dad, I feel awful that he's all alone, so I send him cards. I want to let him know I'm thinking of him always to make him feel better. I want him to feel better. I want to feel better. I send a lot of cards.

Dad is sitting in his wheelchair. His clothing looks and smells like it's been worn for several days. Dandruff flakes fall like snow over the faded red collar of his shirt. Food crumbs from the last several meals trail down his chest like evidence of a dark fairy tale. His hand grips a folded adult diaper. I have to buy his diapers. I have to buy my dad diapers … no wonder I talk to birds.

I take him in and ask when he last showered. He says he showered yesterday, but I'm highly skeptical. Dad refuses to shower regularly, like an uncooperative child. It's so bad that on each visit his nurse du jour begs me to talk him into allowing them to give him a shower. I ask Dad if we could get him showered today.

"Absolutely not."

Up all night buying, washing, and packing clothes that I left at the front desk so they could be embroidered with Dad's details, I'm too tired to argue with Dad about his hygiene. One thing at a time. The theme today is clothing, so I focus on getting him into some clean clothes if I can't get him into the shower.

The clothes I bought last week are back from being labeled and in his strange piece of industrial furniture that serves as a makeshift closet. I show Dad his options, ask him to choose a shirt and pair of pants. Dressing Dad takes half an hour due to his weakness and inability to do just about anything for himself. He can barely stand, even with my help, which makes changing clothes ... difficult. Definitely not a distinguished elderly Ken doll.

Undressing and dressing Dad leaves me embarrassed for both of us. At the same time, his dementia is a mixed blessing at moments like this. He doesn't have the presence of mind to be embarrassed for himself. I suppose I'm embarrassed for the man he used to be. That man would have been aghast that his daughter has to dress him, that his daughter has to buy him diapers.

Today he is holding a spare diaper, but last weekend I found him sitting in his wheelchair wearing *only* his diaper. He was unfazed and looked directly at me like it was totally normal for his adult daughter to see him naked but for a diaper. I should be grateful that Dad doesn't realize his dementia is robbing him of his dignity, but it's also robbing me of my dwindling childhood innocence. It's robbing me of my dad.

With Dad dressed in clean clothes, I gently brush his hair with the little plastic brush provided by the nursing home. Once those tasks are done, while Dad is sitting in his wheelchair, I remove myself to the corner of his room to sit for a visit. The only seat in his room is a hard-ass wooden accent chair that feels more like a punishment than guest furniture. I wonder how much a replacement would cost me at Goodwill and cringe. Still, I may need to bring a comfortable chair because this shit is ridiculous.

We silently stare at the TV I brought from his home, neither of us registering what is happening on the screen or in the room. Dad is too far gone, and I am engaged in mental time travel, turning back the dial a few years before we went over this precipice. My mind wanders, and my heart wishes that I could return to when I didn't have to watch Dad lose his mind before he lost control of his faculties.

My mind begins to drift, and a peaceful feeling washes over me and evokes a gentle smile as I recall my most recent improv class at Theatre 99. My level 2 teacher is Andy, who is just as warm and hilarious as Josh, my level 1 teacher. Having been surrounded by so many unfamiliar faces, both in elder care and improv, the serendipitous consistency of their bald and bearded appearances made me feel at ease. Two nights before, Andy provided prompts—basic emotions like happy, angry, and scared—for us to explore with our created characters.

Then we expressed the change in the character's mood, based on the prompts given by Andy, by adapting their gait and demonstrating how they carried different emotions. Our character walks were meant to teach us how to bring our characters out of our heads and into our bodies, preparing us to embody and express characters in improv scenes in the future.

Learning how to create and embody a character in front of Andy and my classmates made me feel self-conscious. Level 1 was fun, focused on the fundamentals of improv, but level 2 is upping the vulnerability ante. When Andy changed the emotion prompt to "sad," a frown slid down my lips and dripped onto my shoulders, dragging them into a sunken slump. This posture was too easy, bolstered by recent months watching Dad shrivel into the shell of a man he had become.

So I channeled all the inner sadness I'd struggled to suppress, and before I knew it, I was barely able to hold myself up, staggering like a ninety-year-old woman, which is certainly how I felt lately. The frown on my face deepened into a grimace of utter despair, tears filled my eyes, and a guttural moan erupted from my mouth. I allowed myself to fully embody the sorrow that had been my constant companion in the recent months. This was a cathartic release I could have experienced no other way.

Momentarily delivered from this emotional burden, I was able to bounce right into Andy's next prompt, the excited character, skipping instead of walking, jumping up and down with joy, and a big ol' smile lighting up my face. At that moment I fell in love with character work and deeper in love with improv. Putting on new characters like costumes and creating physical movements for each one was a paradox of escaping my mind by being inside my body. This character transformation lets me pause time and step outside my identity of a heartbroken daughter watching her father fade before her eyes.

In the dimly lit theater, surrounded by my classmates, I found solace in the simple act of becoming someone else. And as I danced my way through the rest of the exercise, I was reminded that even in the midst of darkness, there are moments of lightness and joy to be discovered.

I drift back to the present and ask Dad what he's thinking about. He turns to me to respond, and for a beat I recognize him again. I think he understands my question and is on the edge of a profound response. Instead, he turns his head back toward the television and continues to stare.

Usually, Dad's roommate's TV is blaring, decimating any silence in the space he shares with Dad. But Charlie has COVID-19 and is in the quarantine ward for fourteen days. Typically, I'm annoyed that Charlie's TV is so loud, but today the silence feels too heavy. I wonder if Charlie, after surviving all these years, will make it through the latest edition of COVID-19.

Dad and I endure two more hours of silent staring at the television in our respective chairs. Obviously, Dad either doesn't care or doesn't understand that I'm here, and I'm exhausted. When I decide to go, I gather up some of Dad's old clothes, now much too big for him. Maybe I will take them to Goodwill, where they will be bought by another lost daughter for another diminishing father. Lost in my chores, I hear a nurse enter the room; then Dad starts talking.

"Can you please find a bed for my daughter to sleep in tonight so she can stay the night with me?" Dad asks.

Tears I've been holding back all day sting my eyes before flooding over my cheeks. The nurse explains to Dad that I can't sleep there. To buffer his disappointment, I bend over Dad's wheelchair and hug him tightly. I tell him that next weekend I'll get a hotel room here in Walterboro and stay the night so we can spend more time together. I tell him I love him before I hurry out of the room so he won't see me sobbing.

JUNE 9, 2022

It's my forty-fourth birthday. Mired in emotional exhaustion because the most important person in my life, who was actually there the day I was born, has become a shell of himself, I have zero interest in celebrating. I'm amazed that I still have a job after the amount of time I've had to take off this year to care for Dad.

Now they are letting me "work from home," which really means working from "the home," or my car, or wherever I am that is not our office. My workplace and all the warm people there have been so good to me, and I am beyond grateful for the gift of their patience and support.

I am at home, just wanting to enjoy my birthday in peace. However, my reverie is interrupted when my phone vibrates with a text message. Sara is worried. She knows how down I am and is devastated that it's my birthday and she's out of town. Sara always celebrates my birthday with me, and she's afraid I won't leave the house. She's afraid I will stay in crying the night away. Sara knows me so well, as that is indeed my plan.

"Kimberly and the girls want to take you out; I know they do. Promise me you'll go out with them tonight. Promise me," the text reads.

"I'll think about it," I text back.

Sara knows my soul, and the thing I'm most upset about today is that it is the first birthday of my entire life that I will receive no birthday wishes from a parent. Dad is unable to register the day or the year, so it's unrealistic that he might remember that today is my birthday. Even if he magically remembered, he would never be able to figure out how to call me, despite the fact that I got him a landline and placed instructions on the wall. His new phone is cotton candy pink, the only color available when I ordered it. I still chuckle every time I see it, which is great because I desperately need something to chuckle about when I walk in his room.

I've just set my cellphone back on my desk when it vibrates again. This time with a voice call. I don't want to talk to anyone, but caller

EMBRACE FAILURE AND BE ADAPTABLE

ID says that it's the VVH. That is not a surprise; they call every day. Sometimes it's a staff member calling with an unsettling update on Dad. Sometimes it's Dad himself, crying, confused about something and begging me to come. Even though I dread either scenario, I dutifully press Accept.

"Hello," I say, pausing for the shoe to drop. What flavor of sadness will I be served for my birthday?

"Jaclyn, this is Martha. I'm your father's nurse today. And he's right here, wanting to talk to you," she says warmly.

"OK, great, thank you, Martha," I say, cringing in my office chair, bracing myself.

"Happy Birthday, Jaclyn!" Dad says. I can hear the smile in his voice.

I'm so confused. How on earth could he remember? He doesn't even know what century we are in, let alone the date. Joyful tears stream over my beaming smile. I decide not to look this gift horse in the mouth.

"Thank you so much, Dad! Your call means so much to me," I say, as tears run down my face. I've cried so much the past six months. On the one hand, I can't believe there are any tears left inside me; on the other hand, I'm grateful these tears are sweet rather than bitter.

"Of course, I'm calling you on your birthday. This was the most special day of my life, many years ago. You are the greatest joy in my life, Jaclyn, and I appreciate everything you do for me so much. I hope you know that." This makes me cry harder.

"There is one other thing I'd like to talk to you about," Dad continues, suddenly sounding very serious. "These nurses around here are handling me like a piece of meat, Jaclyn, and I'm tired of it. I'm telling you, Jaclyn, these nurses are meat handlers. Meat handlers!" Dad exclaims.

I start laughing, as quietly as possible, and tell him I understand and I'll talk to the nurses about their meat handling when I'm there this weekend. Realistically, I'm more likely to be talking to him about his bathing, but I keep that to myself.

Before we hang up, I can hear him say to the nurse, "I'm done now; please take this phone out of my hand right now."

I shake my head, smiling, and set the phone back down on my desk. I have no idea how that phone call happened, but my heart is radiating from the happiness that it brought. I pick the phone back up, and I text my friend Kimberly: "I think I'm up for a small celebration tonight. Can we go to Jackrabbit Filly for dinner and then Stems and Skins for vinyl night? I want to bring one of Mom's records to play."

"Yes. YAY!! I'll pick you up at 6:30," Kimberly replies.

A few hours later, I climb into Kimberly's SUV, and we head to my favorite Charleston restaurant, Jackrabbit Filly, which happens to be conveniently located in my neighborhood, Park Circle. I've lived in Park Circle for about four years now and am still enamored with its warm, eclectic hippy vibe and incredible sense of community. The small-scale downtown area, just a couple of streets, is packed with charming bars, restaurants, and shops.

We settle into a huge corner booth at Jackrabbit Filly, where I'm surrounded by some of my favorite women—Kimberly, Nina, Tammi, Alia, and Beth. We raise a toast to another trip around the sun for me, and we eat and eat until we can't eat anymore. Heady with the pleasure of good food and good company, I thank God for these women, who lift me up when I need them the most. I'm the luckiest person in the world.

After dinner we head over to Stems and Skins, which became my favorite hangout spot during the pandemic. Thursday nights are vinyl nights when patrons are encouraged to bring a vintage record of their

EMBRACE FAILURE AND BE ADAPTABLE

choice to play for the crowd. Even though it's just around the corner and I've been there often, somehow I've never made it to Stems and Skins for vinyl night. This night has been on my to-do list for ages, especially since I recently acquired Mom's extensive vinyl collection.

Inside the dimly lit bar, I'm transported to another place, which is what I love so much about Stems and Skins. I'm not in my neighborhood; instead I'm in a sexy candlelit bar in Barcelona. The record player spins, belting sultry tunes out of the speakers; the room is drenched in the scent and flavors of wine with the salty undercurrent of a massive cured Spanish ham leg, ready for the cutting, resting on the counter behind the bar.

My favorite sommelier, Rachel, greets me with a warm embrace, telling me how happy she is that I'm there. She knows what's going on with Dad. Rachel always has sweet, kind things to say whenever I see her. She knows the perfect drink; she has the perfect words.

We six ladies surround a long, candlelit table. I sit on the end, taking in these beautiful humans. We order a couple of bottles of sparkling rosé, my favorite, which Rachel delivers before we can drain a single glass of water. After the pour, we all raise our glasses and toast again. We toast to my birthday, to our friendships, and to the future. I have a future, and it is worth toasting.

In this moment, with these women twinkling in the candlelight, supporting me and loving me, I am alive and drinking in life, drinking it deeply, and I'm drunk on the feeling of their love. This magic is just as intense as my grief, and I realize that it's moments like these and the memories that we are making that will see me through the living nightmare of suffering with Dad. I pause to burn it into my mind so I can remember it forever.

Rachel stops by our table again, and I hand her Mom's Rolling Stones record, *Through the Past Darkly*, from 1969. She smiles, instinctively reading that this record is special to me. After she leaves, I turn to my ladies and tell them I want to play a little game.

Recently Alia, one of the other single ladies at the table, and I had joked about how completely different our taste in men is. I tell Alia to take a long look around the bar and find the man she finds the most attractive—the one she would take home tonight … if she were that type of gal, and I'll choose the man I would take home … if I were that type of gal. Then we will guess whom each chose.

Alia and I each size up the room, choosing our lucky hypothetical suitors. Once we agree we've found our Romeos, it's time to guess. I zero in on the very end of the bar and point directly to the preppy-looking man in his thirties. His haircut is impeccable. His clothes are straight out of *GQ*, not Goodwill.

"Him," I say confidently to Alia as the other ladies listen intently, waiting for Alia to confirm or deny that the man I've pointed to is her pick.

Alia begins to laugh, confirming that this man, out of all the fish in this swanky sea, is indeed her choice. Then Alia points to the opposite end of the bar, to the man sitting two seats in from the end. Tall, broad shouldered, dark hair peeking out from under a local brewery hat, he's wearing a black button-down shirt, dark jeans, and boots. And he has a beautiful thick, dark beard, with hints of gray that are barely betrayed by the flickering candlelight.

"That's who you think I'd take home tonight, if I were that kind of girl?" I ask Alia.

She nods, remaining confident in her decision.

"Well, you're damn right; that's my pick." I say, laughing. God, it feels good to laugh again.

All the other ladies begin to laugh, and I'm again taken aback by the forgotten but familiar feel of joy. I haven't felt this good or laughed

EMBRACE FAILURE AND BE ADAPTABLE

this much in more than six months. I didn't know I was capable of levity, with the heavy weight of my life. I glance over at the bar and notice the guy I chose is looking at me, so I innocently smile at him. Then I not so innocently think, "Hmm, maybe I still got it."

My lustful wondering is broken by "Paint It Black," by the Rolling Stones, erupting from the speakers across the bar. Strong and rich vibrations crackling faintly from the record player needle bring my mother back to life. Mom's record setting the soundtrack this perfect night. How fucking cool is this moment? Dad remembered my birthday, my friends are feeding my soul, and now I feel Mom all around me. Nina raises a glass for us all to clink.

"To your mom," Nina says. "And your dad." They know me. They feel me.

We clink our glasses, and I wish moments like this could be preserved like flowers to keep forever, for when I need them. A couple more songs play from Mom's record while mini conversations break out between the ladies. Beth and I are chatting about how things are going with our jobs when my favorite Rolling Stones song, "She's a Rainbow," begins to play, and a sensation takes me.

Of course, I am already buzzing from the good wine, the mood, and the conversation, but something more is happening. This strange feeling is overtaking my body, taking a hold of me; my body and mind are swept up in it, and it brings me to my feet.

I stand up, right in the middle of my conversation with Beth, who looks on in confusion. I don't look back; my attention is laser focused on the man at the bar. I chose him for a hypothetical game, but now things are getting real. I glance back at Beth and say, "I have to go talk to him."

"Who?" Beth is even more confused.

"My pick ..." I say, my words trailing behind me as I walk toward the tall, bearded man sitting at the bar with a friend.

In my wake I hear Beth gasp and say, "What? We don't do that!" But by the time she finishes, I'm already standing next to the man.

I stand next to him for a moment, pretending to need something from Rachel, who is behind the bar. The magnetic pull got me on my feet but stopped short of giving me an opening line. Standing there, so close to him, I have no clue what I'm doing because I do not approach men, period. Words failing me, I order another bottle for the table, chatting with Rachel, pretending rosé is the only reason I'm standing there, pretending the blush rising in my cheeks is only because of the wine. I don't know what I am doing, but I'm waiting for something to happen.

I feel him watching me, so I slowly turn to the right, to face him.

"Is this your record?" the man asks, looking into my eyes.

"It was my mom's record," I say, smiling.

"I love it. I was going to bring a Rolling Stones album tonight but accidentally left it at home," he says.

Wow, I think. I nod. I blink. I wonder ... what do I say next?

"Is it your birthday?" he asks.

"Yes, how did you know?" I say, pretending to be the confident, dream version of myself. I'm dreaming after all.

"Well, you and your girls walked in here with a certain amount of energy and excitement that just led me to believe that was the case," the man says. "And I may have been watching you a bit, and I saw you all toast to your birthday," he says, grinning like he's revealed a secret that he's excited to reveal. And I'm excited he revealed it.

"I'm Jaclyn," I say, over the soundtrack to this dream movie I'm starring in ...

EMBRACE FAILURE AND BE ADAPTABLE

"She comes in colors everywhere, she combs her hair, she's like a rainbow …"

"I'm Dylan … very nice to meet you," my tall, dark, and handsome hypothetical suitor says with a slight twang of a southern accent.

Oh, can this night please never end! Then like a needle scratch, awkward Jaclyn wakes back up and says, "I hope you have a great evening; I've got to get back to my friends."

I turn and walk back to my table of friends, who have been intensely watching the exchange between this new man, Dylan, and me.

"Well, that came out of nowhere! What's gotten into you, Ms. Smith?" Alia laughs as I take my seat.

All the ladies look to me for an explanation. All I can say is, "I don't know what happened. I just had to go talk to him for some reason." (Later, I concluded that Mom was behind all this.)

"Good for you!" Tammi says, raising her glass up in the air again, then tipping it my way.

I glance over at Dylan, who is glancing back at me at this exact moment. We both smile and look away. I go on chatting with the ladies until Alia and Tammi announce that they have to head home for the evening. I stand to hug Alia tightly, thanking her for being there tonight, telling her how much it means to me. As I stand waiting for Tammi to work her way down the table for her hug, I see Dylan coming toward our table, right to me.

I quickly hug Tammi goodbye and laugh at the fact that she has eyes the size of saucers over this male interloper. And then I pull Dylan off to the side for a shred of privacy in this busy bar. I hand him my business card, which has my cell phone number on it. I'm still playacting confident Jaclyn, pretending that I've not been holding the card since the moment I returned to the table, praying I'd find the courage to give it to him.

"You should call me," I say, looking at him and smiling.

"I will," he says. "But I have to tell you right off the bat that I don't live here full time." The look on his face tells me he is wondering if I'm about to change my mind.

"That'll be just fine," I say.

JUNE 11, 2022

I walk into Dad's room, bracing myself as usual. Today Dad sits in his wheelchair in front of the mirror attached to the sink, in the common area he and Charlie share. He looks at his reflection, and his head is slightly lowered so I can't see his face. He sees me, though, and I hear him declare that he has a surprise for me. The tinge of positivity in this interaction is enough to disarm me. It's been so long since he has said something positive to me in person. It's been so long since he's said anything even normal, and I'm so grateful for it.

Dad raises his head just enough that I can see his reflection in the mirror. Since last weekend he's grown a goatee, which is something I've never seen in my forty-four years on this earth. Hell, until six months ago, I had never seen Dad with a lick of facial hair. Since then, he's been rocking a serious beard. He can't exactly shave and won't allow anyone to shave him … or bathe him.

Honestly, I've enjoyed the beard. I think he's looked incredibly handsome with it, you know, when food isn't stuck in it. But a goatee? This is new, and I'm digging it!

"Dad," I say, "You are so handsome!"

Dad turns to me and smiles. I didn't realize how much I've missed his smile. My whole heart smiles right back at him. A gorgeous gray is threaded through in his goatee and matches his perfectly coiffed hair. It looks like it's been recently washed and brushed. He's wearing my favorite of the shirts I recently got him. I'd like to think he wore it on purpose, knowing I was coming to visit. With this mood he's set, it doesn't feel like I'm indulging in magical thinking. It seems entirely plausible that he's done this for me. I'm amazed that he put in this effort and came back to himself long enough to drape himself in vibrant blue-and-orange plaid. Another moment worth remembering.

Dad turns back to the mirror to admire himself again, and he looks proud. I share in his pride, and then he asks me to take a photo of him with my cell phone. I'm thrilled for the chance to do so.

Dad's top front teeth recently fell out, and he is aware enough in this lucid moment to discreetly smile without betraying his gums. His close-mouthed smile and goatee give him a slightly mysterious look, like he has something up his sleeve.

I tell Dad I have a surprise for him too. Then I pull several containers of sushi out of the cooler bag hanging over my arm.

"Shushi!" Dad excitedly exclaims, mispronouncing it like he's always done, which I now find endearing.

Sushi has been my family's favorite food for the last twenty years. Many of my more recent favorite family memories took shape in a Myrtle Beach sushi bar called Miyabi. I find a plastic fork and knife in Dad's room and begin cutting each piece of sushi in half. Dad still has some issues with swallowing.

From my cooler bag, I retrieve a paper plate and two small saucers. Then I serve up the sushi and soy sauce. I push Dad from the common area in his room up to the hospital table that usually hovers over Dad's hospital bed. I set his plate on it and tell Dad I think we should forgo chopsticks this time and just eat with our fingers.

He agrees, smiling. I retreat with my plate to the uncomfortable wooden chair in the corner of the room and grab the remote to the TV. I flip through until I find an Atlanta Braves game, our team. We eat to the accompaniment of the familiar and comforting sounds of the crack of the bat and the cheers from the crowd. Glancing up from my plate, I enjoy Dad enjoying his sushi. This is the best time I've spent with Dad this entire year. Here we are in a place neither of us ever wanted to be, being ourselves and enjoying two of our favorite things: sushi and baseball.

While Dad is relatively lucid, I decide to take advantage of this magical afternoon and ask him some basic questions about his past and his childhood before it's all gone. He spits rapid-fire random facts at me, each a seed to a fading memory. He shares details of his naval service, his parents' marriage, and the more prestigious ancestors we shared.

He also tells me, "I loved going on Signs of Spring walks with you as a child, on the lake we lived by, in Richmond, Virginia. We would walk around the edge of the lake looking at little things sprouting up."

His words tumble out, one unfinished thought after another, and I'm keenly aware how important this conversation is, how precious this information is for us. Diligently, I capture every single word he utters like my life depends on it. Really, his life depends on it, or at least the memory of his life. I know this is my final opportunity to ever hear this information, and I treasure it as much as the air we breathe together in this sacred moment.

DEVELOP YOUR CHARACTER AND PLAY WITH JOY

Improv is all about discovery and exploration, both for your character and for yourself as a performer. Approach each scene with a sense of curiosity and wonder, allowing yourself to be open to anything. Enjoy the process of discovery, embracing the unexpected twists and turns that arise with the creative possibilities that emerge along the way.

After the break-in at my childhood home, we moved into a beautiful two-story redbrick house with navy-blue shutters, smack-dab in the middle of a Marietta neighborhood called West Hampton. A large magnolia tree regally towered over our front yard and gifted us enormous waxy white springtime blooms and the heady scent of sweet southern musk in the heat of the Georgia summers.

Just off the street sat the mailbox that I would later not-so-gracefully run over when I was learning to drive. After that we had a family song to the tune of Alan Jackson's "Don't Rock the Jukebox" but titled

"Don't Hit the Mailbox," which we sang at all special family occasions for years to come. It was a stick shift, people. Cut me some slack.

Marietta was a great place to finish my formative years. Dad loved that word ... *formative* ... and it still makes me laugh because it sounds so serious. Just beyond our neighborhood was a shopping center with a Kroger grocery store and a Subway sandwich shop. Until I was fifteen years old, this piece of strip mall was my beacon of freedom, as it was the only place I was allowed to go alone until I could drive.

At the edge of the neighborhood, near the beautiful entrance lined with seasonal flowers, were an impressive community pool, four tennis courts, and a playground. Directly across the street from the pool lived a little girl named Corinne, who was six months older than I was and would become one of the most important people in my life, and the first brick in the chosen family of my future.

We met in Mrs. Ellerbee's third-grade class, which I joined in the middle of the year, having just left Richmond. I'd never lived anywhere else and was petrified of my new school full of strangers. Corinne was at least a foot shorter than I was (as were most kids my age), and she had an athletic body and skin that somehow managed to hold a tan all year round. Still, this gorgeous creature with her long, sun-kissed blond hair and her huge smile that could light up any room chose to be my friend.

Corinne took me under her wing both at school and in our neighborhood, introducing me to other kids and helping me feel at ease. Through our friendship, we grew to be more like sisters, and our parents would also become forever friends. I spent a lot of time at Corinne's house as a kid. Her mom was a middle-school teacher and was much stricter than mine was. She ran her house like she ran her classroom, with order and discipline and also a ton of love.

Corinne's mom taught me how to be more disciplined with my diet and my studies.

Corinne's dad was a warm and outgoing jokester who was always telling jokes that made me laugh to no end. Corinne's dad taught me how to deliver a good one-liner and also how to make the perfect scrambled eggs (it's all about constant stirring and medium heat, people). Meals at Corinne's house were regimented and always contained the perfect ratio of protein, carbohydrates, and the good fats, as if every detail had been plucked straight from the nutritional food pyramid. I often wondered if the food pyramid poster hung somewhere in the house for quick reference.

Even though Corinne's mom was strict with food and most other things and I enjoyed my mom's more laid-back parental approach, sometimes I envied the structure in Corinne's house and wished I had a little more of it at home. At my house, I ate whatever I wanted, whenever I wanted, and so did Corinne when she came over. My parents were both great cooks, and meals were made with love and more concern for flavor than nutritional content. Still, anxious kids love order and knowing what to expect, and Corinne's family was orderly.

Mom drank multiple Coca-Colas a day, her favorite food was fried chicken, and she and Dad rarely ended a day without ice cream. Corinne loved how food focused our house was, though, and she loved to help Mom in the kitchen, especially when she was making her Saturday morning French toast in her old-timey electric skillet.

On Friday nights, our two families met at Pizza Inn or the Mexican restaurant near the Marietta Square. Corinne's older brother, Chris, would sometimes join us, though not often because he was much too cool to hang out with us. Corinne and I stalked the soda fountain making "suicides" by combining every single soda available into one cup. Life didn't get much better than that—listening to

Billy Joel on the jukebox at Pizza Inn, drinking my suicide through a straw in the clear red-plastic Pizza Inn cup, surrounded by all my favorite people.

• • •

My first actual crush hit me in Mrs. Ellerbee's third-grade class. Many of the girls had crushes on Keith, including me. Keith was a real boy, not one of my celebrity crushes from the teen magazines I begged my mom to buy for me. For the record, I was a *Teen Beat*–magazine girl, and my biggest crushes were Kirk Cameron and Donnie Wahlberg from the world's best band, New Kids on the Block.

Keith was taller than the other boys, and so was I. Keith had short brown hair, brown eyes, and a devious little smile that made him look like he was always up to something suspicious. He was cool, and he knew he was cool. I knew I was not cool.

One afternoon just before school got out, a note was passed to me. Written on wide-ruled notebook paper and folded a million times, the note somehow formed a perfect rectangle with a little triangle tab stuck out of the side serving as a pull tab. It was a work of art.

I looked around the room and wondered where this note came from, but everyone's eyes were fixed on Mrs. Ellerbee, who was reviewing our homework assignment for the evening. I figured it must be from Corinne, but my name on the front was not in her handwriting.

After class, I rushed to meet Corinne. Carefully and dramatically, I produced the note from my pocket. After unfolding it with care, I read it aloud.

DEVELOP YOUR CHARACTER AND PLAY WITH JOY

Dear Jaclyn,

I'm happy we are in the same class. I like you very much and want you to be my girlfriend.

From,
Keith

My hands immediately started shaking, and excitement and adrenaline began rushing through my body, making me sweat. Corinne and I started jumping up and down. I had a boyfriend! Keith was my boyfriend! This was the best day of my life!

Corinne and I climbed aboard our school bus and rode the three miles home to our neighborhood. We talked about all the incredible things that would happen to me now because I had a boyfriend. The most important thing was our first kiss, and I started thinking of all the places it could happen. The place that of course first came to mind was under the old metal bleachers out by the football field. But a lot of girls at our school were having first kisses there, and I wanted mine to be more original than that. I'd have to give it some serious thought.

At the dinner table that night, I told my parents that something big had happened that day. I told them that Keith had asked me to be his girlfriend and that this was the happiest day of my life. I had seen boyfriends and girlfriends on TV and in the movies, but I hadn't thought it would happen to me this soon.

After sharing my big news, I sat back and waited for all the congratulations and excitement that were sure to follow. Mom and Dad did not react as I hoped. Instead, they exchanged nervous glances at each other across the table. Mom looked at me with a soft, hopeful smile and said she was happy for me, as long as Keith was a nice boy and treated me right. I assured both Mom and Dad that he was and that he would.

I barely slept that night. Corinne and I were on our Swatch phones (google them; you will not be disappointed) until late in the evening, discussing what I was going to wear for my first official day as Keith's girlfriend. We landed on a dark denim skirt that fell just above my knees and a delicate white eyelet top.

The next morning, I was dressed and accessorized with small gold knotted earrings, my peach-colored Swatch watch, white socks, and white Keds. That day, Dad drove Corinne and me to school and dropped us off at the front door. I waved goodbye to him as I nervously walked into the school, down the hall, and into our classroom, Corinne by my side.

It was a few minutes before class, and I saw Keith chatting with a friend of his. I looked at Corinne, and she assertively motioned for me to go over to him, which I did. I slowly walked over and said hello to Keith, smiling timidly. Keith and his friend stopped chatting and stared at me. I told Keith that I received his note yesterday, and I was excited to be his girlfriend. I then asked if he would like my phone number so he could call me today after school.

Keith looked at me, then at his friend; then a huge smile appeared on his face, followed by uncontrollable laughter. The two boys continued laughing for a couple of minutes while I stared at them, confused. When the laughter finally started to subside, Keith explained to me that the note was a joke and that he definitely did not want me to be his girlfriend. He said that one of his buddies dared him to do it. Then he and his friend turned back to each other and continued their conversation.

I felt like I had been punched in the gut. Hard. I stumbled backward and away from Keith and the other boy. Corinne looked at me from across the room, obviously wanting to know what had just happened, and I opened my mouth to say something, to mouth something across the room at her, but nothing came out. Speechless, I spun around and ran out of that classroom, down the long hallway, and into the bathroom. I spent the next hour sobbing, locked inside the last stall.

When I got home from school that day, I went directly to my room and didn't come out, even when I was told dinner was ready. Dad had prepared BBQ chicken on the grill, but I had no desire to eat. Refusing food was a clear sign to my mom that something was wrong. She knocked on my bedroom door and asked through the door why I wasn't coming down for dinner. I didn't even reply.

Mom slowly opened my bedroom door. She always entered slowly, partly out of respect for my privacy and because opening it at speed would cause a gust that could take out the New Kids on the Block posters and cutouts. Mom found me lying on my bed, hugging my stuffed gray Pound Puppy, Benji. I was listening to my newest New Kids on the Block cassette. She could tell by my puffy eyes I had been crying. When she asked what was wrong, I told her the events of the day.

Mom hugged me tight and told me that life wasn't always fair and that people didn't always do the right thing. She told me that it was up to me to always try to do the right thing and to follow the Golden Rule. (Mom was a huge fan of the Golden Rule: treat others as you want to be treated.) And then she convinced me to come downstairs and have dinner with her and Dad, followed by butter pecan ice cream.

· · ·

Ms. Stratford ruled our classroom with an iron fist. A short, stocky woman, she always wore slacks that were ironed with perfectly crisp creases. Ms. Stratford expected a lot out of her fourth graders, but I struggled to meet her expectations.

Assignment after assignment, Ms. Stratford returned a series of Cs. Occasionally, I got a lucky B. These subpar results left me ridiculously anxious as she stalked up and down each aisle of desks, like a big cat hunting her prey. She handed back our disappointing papers one by one, an evil grin illuminating her face. OK, the evil grin might be creative license on my part, but her disappointment was all too real.

My anxiety was palpable. When Ms. Stratford approached, I pressed my lips tightly together and held my breath, waiting for her to drop the bomb … my paper bleeding red ink and scarred with the letter C. Sometimes my eyes filled with tears, but I was never the only one. The entire classroom felt under attack. My parents were proactive and sat with me as I worked hard on my homework every single night. Still, it was never good enough, and I was never good enough for Ms. Stratford.

No one was more eager to please. I would have done just about anything for an A, something that came so easily to me in third grade. The stress kept me up at night, and when I did sleep, I had nightmares about failing important tests. Once I even dreamed that I was expelled from elementary school for doing so poorly on a paper. My fears manifested physical symptoms with teeth grinding and neck pain so severe my parents had to call in the professionals. Thankfully, Ms. Stratford is now just a terrible memory.

...

Fifth grade presented me with a lovely teacher by the name of Ms. Harper who had kind, light-blue eyes and an easygoing smile. Her demeanor put me at ease. School was always stressful for me because my anxiety started at a young age, but I managed to make a new friend, Lisa, who sat behind me in class.

Lisa's strawberry blond curly hair fell just a bit above her shoulders, and she wore trendy huge octagonal glasses (it was the 1980s). When she got excited and started laughing, the sweet freckles on her face would dance. We struck up a conversation in class one day about boys or something equally silly, and our conversation has never actually ended. It's just "to be continued" in the next episode of a lifelong friendship.

Lisa's neighborhood was a few miles from mine. Sometimes her older brother, Cole, was home and would take us to high school tailgates. Lisa's older sister, Kim, was usually at their house and quickly became the big sister I always wished I had. Even though she was older than both of us, Kim was shorter than Lisa and I were.

Short but beautiful and feisty, Kim was mature and self-assured. Upstairs in their bonus room, Kim hung out with us and never acted like we were bothering her or cramping her style, even though she had every right to resent the intrusion. Instead, we three sat together on the couch, watching the first season of *The Real World* on MTV and paging through *YM* magazine. Feet propped up on the coffee table, we gave ourselves manicures and pedicures while gossiping about our crushes as the smell of nail polish drifted through the air.

I loved Lisa and Kim's noisy home. They had an intercom system that ran throughout each room of the house. It usually belted out solid-gold oldies. If we were really lucky, their parents would pipe old-school country classics from Waylon Jennings or Willie Nelson through the house.

I became close to Lisa and Kim's parents, though their dad intimidated the hell out of me. He was quiet and had a strong presence. His "no bullshit permitted" demeanor was so effective that no one ever tested him. If it was just an act, it was highly effective.

Lisa's mom was a sweet, yet strong woman who also tolerated no bullshit. We did as we were told in the Dickerson household. The house motto was "Pull yourself up by your bootstraps when times get hard." Mrs. Dickerson would often share this pearl of wisdom while she lovingly served her homemade chili and cornbread for us to devour while we sat around the dining room table sharing stories about our days.

Our friendship continued over the years. As we got older, Kim and I got closer too. Nowadays, Lisa and Kim are considered my sisters. It's Corinne, Lisa, Kim, and I (and one more lovely lady I'll introduce to you later) who formed the McGee family.

...

My ride-or-die girls (Corinne, Lisa, and Kim) were always there for me, and I had a few other close friends who stood the test of time: Matt, Missy, and Terra. Still others floated in and out of my life, appreciated in their seasons, but not permanent fixtures. Occasionally, I encountered a questionable but consequential influence like Bailey.

When I was thirteen, Bailey introduced me to my first cigarette, and a nicotine fiend was born. The first puff rushed to my brain, followed by a small cough. The lingering taste was terrible, horrible, disgusting, awful … pure nastiness. But, oh my, the little high that hit my brain at that moment was as intense as the fact that I was knowingly doing something forbidden. The taboo and the buzz were enough to hook me for life, or at least for as long as it took me to finally stop.

We escalated to huffing gasoline, Bailey's idea, but this was a one-time thing, never a habit—at least not for me. When Bailey's mom casually opened the garage door from inside her minivan, her long day at work turned into a long night at home. She found Bailey and me lying nearly unconscious on her garage floor next to an open can of gasoline.

Bailey's mom hovered over us screaming loud enough to wake the dead. We weren't dead, just really high. With her prodding screams, we came to and couldn't really remember why we were lying on the garage floor. When it clicked, we knew we were in big trouble.

Bailey's mom called my mom, who drove over immediately. The expression on Mom's face—the disappointment, the fear—looked like Bailey's mom's scream had sounded. Mom led me to the passenger side of our silver Audi 5000 sedan, opened the door, and guided me inside before shutting the door for me. After she climbed in, Mom drove me home in silence. No radio, no conversation. Just silence.

Later that evening, after I'd had a couple of hours alone in my room, thinking about everything that happened, Mom and Dad called me into the living room to have a conversation. Mom's eyes were swollen, and her nose was stuffed up, like she had been crying.

I explained to them that I had never done anything like that before and I would never do anything like it again. I promised Bailey was the one who wanted to try it, and I went along with her because I didn't want to look uncool. My parents nodded, and Mom told me how dangerous huffing gasoline was and how dangerous drugs were. She told me that I needed to come to them if I was ever tempted to do anything like that again. She told me they'd always be there for me, always, but that I needed to come to them.

Dad told me that my future was way too bright for drugs, and this was a pivotal moment in my life where my decisions would have a much greater impact on my future than before. He said that the decisions I made right now would be the ones that steered the direction of the rest of my life, and I needed to make the right ones. (Did I listen? Of course not. I was thirteen and still high on gasoline fumes.)

Well, a month after the gas-huffing incident, Bailey invited me back. We sat in her room listening to a cassette tape of a new band called the Black Crowes on her pink boom box. Just hanging out being normal thirteen-year-old girls, everything was fine until it wasn't.

Bailey excused herself to go to the bathroom, and I lay back on her twin bed, listening to the *Shake Your Money Maker* album, thinking I'd never heard anything better in my life. Each song was better than the last, but then it occurred to me that Bailey had been in the bathroom for a really long time. Maybe she was smoking and didn't invite me this time.

I flipped through fashion magazines until a deep tension hit my stomach. I felt like—no, I *knew* in my gut—that something was very wrong. I knocked on Bailey's bathroom door, softly at first, then a little harder. I called her name and asked if everything was all right. I was trying to be quiet to not cause Bailey new trouble with her mom. However, with no response, my knocking eventually became pounding with my fists and demanding Bailey open the door. Bailey still didn't respond, but her mother came running down the hall from the other side of the house.

She looked at my concerned face and started banging on the door, too, demanding that Bailey open it. After about thirty incredibly long seconds with no response, Bailey's mother remembered a key to the bathroom balanced on the small ledge over the door. She opened the door to find Bailey slumped over next to her toilet, with blood running down her arm. Blood was everywhere. It was all over her blue plaid shirt and the pale-pink rug she was lying on. Her mom ran to her child to put pressure on her arm, and she instructed me to go to the phone in the kitchen and call 911, which I did. I'd never called 911 before; I'd never seen so much blood in my life.

The 911 operator dispatched emergency responders. When they told me I could hang up, I called Mom. With her mother by her side, Bailey was taken away in an ambulance. My mom arrived and hugged me tight, over and over, while I told her what had happened. I told Mom that I was so confused and couldn't understand why Bailey would want to die, to cut her wrists. I couldn't comprehend how she could inflict that much physical pain upon herself. Mom had tears running down her face, but no easy answers.

Instead, she told me that Bailey obviously had some things she needed to work through, and it was best if I kept a distance for now. We didn't talk too much about it because back then, suicide attempts weren't openly discussed. Even if we didn't talk about it, it was clear that everyone was worried.

Unsure of how to act, I did as Mom said and kept my distance from Bailey. I never went back to her house, and we were never close friends again. I saw her at school every single day, and we'd exchange glances and timid smiles while we both held tight to the secrets we kept for and from each other.

・・・

Not long after the Bailey incidents, I accidentally discovered organized religion. Maybe it was the antidote to the trauma of witnessing Bailey's desperation, but I liked how friendly and inclusive everyone was at Lisa's Southern Baptist church. They welcomed me right in, and before I knew it, I was knee deep into three services per week, youth group meetings, church lock-ins, and choir tours.

We toured malls all over the East Coast, singing about God. Our biggest hit was called "People Need the Lord." It's OK if you laughed. I laughed while typing it.

I loved church life.

And I made a good friend in a girl my age named Claire. Claire was a lot like me—she liked church but also wanted to live on the wild side. Claire had long, curly blond hair, a slender yet curvy frame, and a big pool in her backyard.

One summer, Claire and I spent almost every single day sunbathing at her pool. We'd rub oil all over ourselves and lie on floats in the middle of the pool, chatting about boys and what parties we wanted to go to that weekend. One Saturday night, Claire and I asked to be dropped off at a friend's house, and her mom agreed. We did not tell her it was a party. The air was muggy and foggy, full of Georgia humidity right after a summer rain, and we were ushered inside to a room full of much older teenagers with no questions asked and handed red Solo cups of beer, which I'd never had before. It tasted bitter and gross, and I had to force it down my throat.

Claire didn't seem to have trouble drinking the beer or talking to the other kids at the party. It took me about an hour to get half the beer down, and by the time I did, Claire was nowhere to be found. I didn't have anyone else to talk to, and I felt scared and uncomfortable. Overwhelmed with how uncool I felt, I quietly backed out into the hallway.

I made my way to a screened-in porch, where a good-looking guy with dark brown hair and a red plaid shirt walked over to me and introduced himself as Billy.

He took me by the elbow and led me over to a small glass table in the corner of the porch and pulled a small plastic baggie out of the pocket of his jeans. I stared at the little pouch of white powder he'd retrieved and wondered why Billy was walking around with baby powder in his pocket.

Billy opened the baggie and sprinkled some of the baby powder onto the glass table. He then grabbed his wallet out of his back pocket and pulled out a twenty-dollar bill. He rolled up that bill very tightly, bent over the table, and snorted what was, in fact, not baby powder! He tried to hand me the twenty-dollar bill.

Until that moment, cocaine was something that had only existed in movies. As much as I enjoyed indulging in a little rebellion and crossing some lines, cocaine seemed too serious, too far. I made no movement to accept the twenty-dollar bill, but after about twenty seconds of just staring at Billy, I turned and ran.

Inside the house, I grabbed the kitchen phone, and hiding in a stranger's pantry, I dialed my home phone number. I stood outside for about fifteen minutes on that lonesome, muggy night, scared of what Dad was going to do to me for going to a party and for lying about it.

He and Mom pulled the Audi right up to where I was standing. I climbed inside. I waited for Dad to yell at me. But he didn't. And neither did Mom.

Dad put the car in first gear and slowly pulled forward, exiting the apartment complex parking lot. Mom reached her hand back through the front two seats and grabbed mine. As they took turns telling me that they loved me, that I could always call them, no questions asked, and that they were so happy I called and relieved I was safe, I felt even closer to them emotionally. My faith that they would always be there for me was never stronger. I was blessed with a very special bond with my parents, a bond most kids my age would never be lucky enough to have.

• • •

In the tenth grade I traded in my Bible and youth group gatherings for costumes, the stage, and all things "drama." Corinne and I signed up for our first drama class on a whim (the alternative was PE, no contest).

I loved drama class and our teacher, Ms. Walker. In her bohemian-style dresses and skirts, she encouraged me to be silly and really put myself out there while acting. I loved that I could become someone else entirely when I was playing a character.

Best of all, I loved the fact that on stage I forgot about any trials or tribulations going on in my life. I could focus on only the moment at hand and what my character was doing and saying. I grew more involved in drama and officially joined the drama club, with Corinne in tow. I also immersed myself in the behind-the-scenes work of our high school's drama productions. My interests led to the role of house manager for the annual Harrison High School Talent Show!

Mom and Dad came to see me in all my glory. They brought me a dozen long-stemmed red roses wrapped in cellophane, hugged me tightly, and told me how proud they were of me for my work behind the scenes.

I eventually lettered in drama—did you know that was even possible? (I didn't!)—and was inducted into the National Thespian Society, with Corinne by my side. Drama club was exactly what high-school Jaclyn needed: a safe space where I could be myself without the fear of being judged.

. . .

When I was sixteen, I found a new friend, Monica. She was a high school dropout with short hair that fell a couple of inches above her shoulders, but beneath that hair, the back of her scalp was completely shaved.

Monica wore inappropriate T-shirts; her favorite had two goats having sex, which she wore with extremely short black leather skirts and black fishnet tights. Monica introduced me to a whole new group of inappropriate friends, and Ross was in that group.

Ross was twenty-one and lived with a couple of other guys his age in a single-wide mobile home near Lake Allatoona. Every single weekend, I made up stories about where I was going to hang out with my inappropriate crowd.

I grew closer to Ross and developed a massive crush on him. Of course, at sixteen, I thought I was in love with Ross. A smidge over six feet tall, with dark brown short hair, beautiful olive skin, and a tattoo on his shoulder of a University of Florida gator, Ross was effortlessly cool. His subtle beard was a wonder, whether it was intentional or he had just skipped a few shaves.

Ross and his band played shows all around the Atlanta area, and he always ensured I was on the guest list, which gave me a pass on ID. After his shows, I returned to Ross's mobile home, where we would make out on top of the soft teal-colored blanket on his bed. Ross's dimly lit room smelled sweet like Jack Daniels, with a hint of Budweiser. I was timid and scared, and I don't think Ross and I ever got past first base because he could tell that I was terrified.

I was 100 percent sure that Ross was my soul mate and that I was hopelessly in love with him, but he ended our relationship after a few months. He told me I was just simply too young. I was beyond devastated and didn't get out of bed for a week.

During my week of mourning, I told my parents I had some kind of stomach bug. They humored me, though I know they suspected something. I normally talked to my parents about everything, but this was too difficult to discuss with them. Between Ross's age and the fact that I'd lied to them to spend time with him, I needed to keep this to myself. Instead, I leaned on Corinne and Lisa to get through my first real heartbreak.

. . .

During my wild teenage years, reality hit a little too hard. Mom started dropping weight rapidly, suffering bouts of extreme fatigue and recurring urinary tract infections. One Tuesday afternoon, she went to her primary care provider for tests, and they quickly determined that she had type 2 diabetes.

Her blood sugar was so high that they immediately admitted her to the hospital, where she remained for several days until they were able to get her numbers under control.

After overcoming cancer while giving birth, it seemed that Mom's health issues were historical events, not immediate threats. Now, she had been diagnosed with something serious. Dad would take me to the hospital every day after school, and I'd climb into the bed with my mom, hugging her tightly.

Nurses came in and out of the room and taught Mom how to give herself insulin shots in the stomach, but she wanted no part of it. The nurses would bring in plump, juicy oranges for Mom to practice on, and she would practice stabbing the oranges. When it was time for her to do it on her own stomach, Mom would cry and shake. Mom had a huge fear of needles, and this would be the most challenging thing she had ever had to do.

Mom saw a nutritionist while she was hospitalized. Long gone were the days of Church's fried chicken, endless bowls of ice cream for dessert, and ice-cold Coca-Cola. At least I thought those days were over. They had to be over, right?

Mom was told repeatedly about the dangers of not following a healthy diabetic-management diet and all the horrible health issues that could occur if she did not take her insulin twice a day as prescribed. She would be at a much higher risk for heart disease, stroke, kidney disease … the list went on and on. Mom was scared but tried her best to act calm as she assured the hospital staff and Dad and me that she was taking this seriously.

I could not even start to *think* about anything terrible happening to her. She was my very best friend. Every single night, I would pray to God to please look after Mom and help her to be healthy and make healthy choices. I prayed that God would help her to not buy chips and ice cream at the grocery store on her weekly trips.

Sometimes my mind would wander through all the bad things that could happen to her as a result of diabetes. My eyes would fill with tears, and as the negative, anxious thoughts took over, I would try very hard to slowly breathe in and out, in and out, over and over again. "God, I promise I'll be really good if you could just make sure Mom is OK."

My relationship with my parents was full of unconditional love and care, yet always mixed with just a sprinkle of anxiety for good measure. Anxiety from my parents about my making the right life decisions and also anxiety from me about my parents making the right life decisions.

My biggest fear as a small child was that something bad might happen to my parents. That fear was growing as I got older, along with my swelling anxiety. Looking back on it, my parents and I were fated to ride a codependent roller coaster for many years to come.

TAKE RISKS AND LIVE IN THE MOMENT

Don't be afraid to take risks. Think outside the box with your character choices, even if they seem unconventional. Experiment with bold choices that push the boundaries of what's expected, and trust that your instincts will guide you in the right direction. By living in the moment and remaining present, you can respond authentically to what is happening in the scene in real time.

JULY 18, 2022

When I walk out of the San Francisco airport, I try my best to channel that confident energy I had on my birthday when I met Dylan. Instead of overthinking everything, I've formed no expectations of what this trip and what this relationship is going to be. When Dylan asked me to meet him in California to spend the week with him, driving down the Pacific Coast Highway, yes seemed like the only appropriate answer.

In the few weeks I've known Dylan, I've learned that he has a condominium in Charleston about twenty minutes from where I live. He keeps most of his belongings in his itty-bitty hometown located in the upstate of South Carolina, where his family still resides. Dylan's grandfather coincidentally lives in the same nursing home as my dad. South Carolina is not a huge state, but what are the chances that the cute guy I met in my favorite bar on my birthday would share that connection?

Dylan uses his grandfather's vacant house to store all his worldly belongings because he's unsure of where he wants to buy an actual house. He's unsure of where he wants to make a home. The third of Dylan's dwellings is his state-of-the-art camper/toy hauler. This vehicle is built to withstand the coldest of temperatures and be pulled through whatever muddy situations an outdoorsy person may find themselves navigating. Dylan stores his camper in a private location in Southern Colorado, where it patiently awaits Dylan for his next Western adventures.

I was immediately drawn to Dylan's sense of adventure and love of traveling. Though I've been fortunate enough to gallivant around Europe a few times, lately I've felt the urge to get out and explore the good old US of A more. I couldn't believe my luck. A cute, bearded guy who smells amazing, likes me, and also loves to travel? Sign me up!

Of course, my safety was a valid concern. I'd only known this man for a few short weeks, and joining him in his camper for a week caused some concern, especially for Corinne. She insisted on conducting a complete background check, which he passed with flying colors. Then she demanded I download a tracking app so she could monitor a little Jaclyn dot moving down the West Coast.

As I look for Dylan's truck, my nerves poke through my numbness like the pokey ends of feathers through a soft cushion. One thought after another pricks my consciousness. What am I doing here? What if he murders me, dumps my body in the Pacific Ocean, and I end up as a story on *Dateline*?

TAKE RISKS AND LIVE IN THE MOMENT

Images of *Dateline* correspondents interviewing my BFFs fade to the back of my mind as I see a big white GMC heading my way. The truck's lights are flashing off and on, over and over, making quite a spectacle. That's my Dylan, grinning from ear to ear in the driver seat as he guides the truck to a stop right in front of me. He jumps out, walks around the front of the truck, leans down to kiss my lips, grabs my suitcase, and tosses it casually in the back of the truck.

I hop up into the passenger seat and watch him confidently ease himself into the driver's seat and steer us out of the airport into beautiful downtown San Francisco. While Dylan drives us through the winding streets of San Francisco, I stare, gobsmacked, at all the brightly colored Victorian houses. I've finally made it to California, a place that until this day, I was skeptical really existed outside of TV and movies. The scenery is competing for my attention with the scent of Dylan sitting next to me. I'm easily distracted by this smell that is so intoxicatingly male—clean soap layered on a woodsy fragrance with hints of hair product and manly sweat.

We make our way to the old Ferry Building right on the water to have dinner at the Hog Island Oyster Company. This is just one of Dylan's many favorite restaurants located all over the country. He is always finding himself on an adventure from one state to another, usually in search of new motorcycles or dirt bikes to purchase.

Dylan and I are bar-sitting kinds of people, so we take our place at the bar at Hog Island Oyster Company. I try to avoid staring at him like a sixteen-year-old girl ogling her crush. I'm smitten with this man, and I can't help but think Mom orchestrated this whole thing from beyond the veil. After all, it was her record playing when something took over my entire body and led me over to talk to him on my birthday. It had to be her. Did she send me my forever person? God, I hope so.

Dylan orders for us, as he often does, and soon raw oysters on the half shell appear in front of us, with lemon, mignonette, and cocktail sauces. I never enjoyed raw oysters before Dylan, but now I love them. Dylan has elevated all my tastes by sharing many of the finer things in life, such as good wine. Really good wine. We sip on a delicate, crisp rosé as we tip one oyster after another into our mouths. Then our steamer bowls arrive, packed to the brim with fresh clams, braised greens, and fennel sausage.

The steamer bowl is insanely good, but I only eat half of it because I am nervous about my stomach, which has been doing somersaults all day. Even though I am not overthinking with my brain, my stomach is clearly anxious about this trip with this beautiful man I barely know. It doesn't help that I will also be in a strange bathroom situation in his camper this evening, and I am extremely nervous about that.

Dylan has reassured me over and over again that the camper has a bathroom with a toilet I can use, but I know the camper is small. He'll probably be able to hear and smell everything, so how am I supposed to go number two in there? I barely know this man, and I'm still trying to give the illusion that I'm a hot piece of ass who doesn't go number two or anything else gross like that.

Dylan asks for the check and hands over his credit card before I can even open my purse. I'm grateful, though. Dad's expenses keep piling up, and unlike Dylan, whose home away from home is a camper, I've been staying in a Myrtle Beach Hampton Inn, which, after nearly three months, is competing with my actual home for my largest expense.

We leave the bar hand in hand. I love holding this man's hand. When we make it to the truck, we hop up in, and before he starts the ignition, I lean over, tenderly kiss him, thanking him for dinner and for bringing me to California. He kisses me back, and I can't wait to get my arms around this sexy fella when we get to the camper ... until I see the camper.

We drive a little more than an hour north to Napa, where Dylan now pulls the truck up to his camper, sitting there in all its glory. Sage green with industrial black trim, the trailer is the size of an en-suite bathroom and nested among twenty other campers of various sizes and colors. Dylan looks back at me for a reaction to his beautiful bundle of joy.

"I love it," I say with a nervous smile, wondering how on earth we are going to coexist in this tiny thing for a week. I gingerly climb the retractable metal stairs and step into Dylan's green machine. It's narrow as hell, and the first thing I notice is the kitchen, which consists of a small fridge, a couple of stove burners over a small oven, and a sink.

My eyes wander left of the kitchen to a cushioned bench long enough to seat two people next to a wall-mounted folding table. My eyes dart past the bench to ... a bed? Yes, it's a double-sized bed suspended in midair. Dylan excitedly heads over to the bench and shows me how to get into the bed, by stepping up onto the bench and hoisting oneself up into the bed, which is literally in the air.

"Isn't this great?" Dylan asks me, with the expression of a kid on Christmas morning or at least a kid showing off his new bunk bed at a sleepover.

"Absolutely," I lie, my stomach cramping right then and there at the thought of getting out of *that* bed in the middle of the night to use the bathroom.

Dylan hops down from the bed up in the air and excitedly tells me that the bed lifts flush to the ceiling to store his motorcycle. The motorcycle goes right up a ramp, into the back of the camper, in the area of the bed in the air, not to be confused with an air bed. An air bed would seem normal.

Dylan directs me to the other end of the camper and the tiniest bathroom I've ever laid eyes on. I've used larger airplane bathrooms, but somehow this one also has a tiny shower along with the toilet and sink.

"You can just do whatever you need to do in this toilet, OK? You don't need to worry about a thing," he says with a caring smile.

I nod, and then Dylan grabs a bottle of Chenin Blanc out of the fridge and pours us two glasses. Dylan tells me that there are also public restrooms here, just around the corner from the camper, should I want to use one of those. "Options," I think to myself, wondering which toilet I'll choose and when.

Dylan and I cozy up on the small bench in the "living room" area of the camper and toast to a trip to remember. Our conversation covers our itinerary: We're going to hang in Napa for a bit tomorrow, then head down the coast to Big Sur, which I'm eager to see. From there, we'll make our way down to Paso Robles and spend a couple of days riding his motorcycle and touring wineries.

After California, we'll head east, over to southern Colorado, and spend a day or two in the little town he calls his home away from home. Then he'll drop me off at the little airport in a town called Alamosa, and I'll fly to Denver, then home to Charleston.

I'm a long way from the Dad troubles I've been dealing with the past seven months, and I couldn't be happier about that. What an incredible distraction!

Good and buzzed on wine, we finish planning our week, and Dylan heads to the bed in the air. Before I vault into the bed to join him, I retrieve a sexy piece of lingerie that I packed for this occasion (I'm no dummy). My sexy feelings are bruised as I awkwardly bump against the walls of the tiny bathroom putting on my sexy nighty. Then I have to climb into the bed in the air, with Dylan's assistance, of course, and scooch all the way over to the wall, which is not far at all. Dylan climbs back up into the bed after me. What happens next is pixelated; this isn't that kind of book. When my story becomes a TV show or movie, I'll be happy to dish out those hot little details for you.

Dylan drifts off to sleep really fast, as men usually do. Then the snoring begins like a freight train rattling the trailer. Try as I may to fall asleep, I can't escape the snoring sharing this double bed when I'm used to being the queen of my own king bed.

Right on schedule, my stomach begins to turn. Is it the rich seafood dinner or just my nerves or both? Then I realize I'm literally *trapped* in this bed in the air. I cannot get out without waking Dylan to get down and let me out, and ... I can't do that. That would be mortifying.

I lie there another fifteen minutes until I feel like I may poop my pants. Pooping my pants would be a much worse way to wake Dylan, so I finally nudge him. Sweetly, I say, "Hey babe, wake up, I need to get out of the bed. I have to go to the bathroom."

He comes to and jumps up immediately, even though he's disoriented from being sound asleep. "Are you OK?" he asks.

"Yep, no big deal at all, my stomach is just a little upset," I fib.

I maneuver myself from the bed to the bench to the floor and realize how badly I need to go to the bathroom. I cannot—will not—do it in the tiny bathroom just a few feet away from the bed in the air within earshot and smell-shot of the man I'm crazy about.

"I'm actually going to go to the public bathroom around the corner," I say, pretending to be calm and not as scared to go out into the night as I actually am.

Like a gentleman, he offers to walk me there, but I insist I've got it. Dylan caves and hands me his headlamp, sighing with slight frustration, "Put this around your head."

I put the headlamp around my head and adjust the scratchy Velcro straps. Dylan leans toward me, and I think he's about to kiss me, but instead he turns the light on. Disappointed, I look down and realize I'm in a very sexy piece of lingerie, and that's it. I grab a long cardigan sweater from my suitcase, slip on some boots, and tell Dylan to go back to bed, saying I'll be back shortly.

I open the camper door and walk out into the night, in search of those bathrooms Dylan showed me earlier. I get lost, of course, because why wouldn't I? I come close to actually shitting myself before I finally find the bathrooms. I open the door to a public bathroom stall not unlike one you'd find in a gas station or rest stop. Beggars can't be choosers, and I do what I need to do.

A lifetime of anxiety-fueled digestion means I brought my vape pen to ease my nerves. Here I sit in a sketchy public bathroom, clinging to nicotine, wearing sexy black lingerie accessorized with a man's sweaty headlamp and boots. My stomach is really upset, and I doubt I can leave the bathroom because I know I'll end up right back in here. I just have to laugh so I don't cry.

I start texting a couple of my girls, informing them that I'm safe in CA but that my stomach is not safe, and I tell them about the situation at hand. I even take a photo of myself and send it out to the girls, looking forward to their waking up to the epic photo in the morning. After a half hour, I finally have my stomach under control. When I open the door to the bathroom, Dylan's standing there, waiting for me.

I can only imagine what he thought as he put his arm around me and walked me back to the camper.

"Are you all right?" he asks, genuinely concerned.

"Yep," I say. "Sorry about all this."

"It's no problem. I just want you to be OK," he says.

As we approach the camper, I pause for a moment and look down at my outfit. Dylan does the same, and we both burst out laughing.

JULY 28, 2022

I dramatically raise my glass of sparkling rosé and clink glasses with Corrin, a coworker of mine I've been dying to hang out with since I met her. We just clicked, and it didn't hurt that she shares a name with one of my BFFs. I admire Corrin's intellectual prowess and her insanely quick wit. Her humor flies through the air like an arrow and lands exactly right, every single time. Corrin has me in fits of laughter whenever we talk, and even more so tonight, over drinks and raw oysters at a hip local restaurant in Charleston.

Light and airy are both the wine we're delicately sipping and our lively conversation. This is precisely what I need tonight. We talk briefly about work but mostly about my new man and my recent trip to California. I'm desperate to keep my mind off Dad, who's been struggling even more than usual the past couple of weeks.

One of my biggest fears since Dad entered the nursing home is that he will contract COVID-19, and alas, he finally has. Dad was sent back to the quarantine unit for fourteen days and was moved back to his regular room a few days ago, after a negative COVID-19 test. Leaving quarantine was an immense relief, but unfortunately the virus took its toll on Dad. His already frail body returned another ten pounds lighter. Weaker than he's ever been, completely unable to move around his room without help from a nurse or aide, Dad is now 100 percent incontinent. These are the thoughts I do *not* want to entertain.

Instead, I'm drinking up every moment of this beautiful evening, feeling light as a feather, free from all responsibilities and demands. Then I see my cell phone light up with a phone call … from the Veterans' Victory House.

Bad Daughter is first on the scene: "Do I *have* to answer this? I'm sure it's nothing serious, and I'm having such a lovely evening. I'm sure it's just a nurse calling to tell me Dad is requesting Stetson aftershave, which he recently did, and then used the entire bottle in one week … it can wait."

Good Daughter is having none of it and metaphorically slaps the shit out of Bad Daughter. I answer the call the way only Good Daughter can. "Hello?" I say.

"Hi, Jaclyn, this is Mia from the Veterans' Victory House. I'm calling to let you know that your dad fell out of his bed this evening, resulting in some injuries, and he is currently being taken by ambulance to a hospital in Charleston."

"What? Oh my God. Is he OK? What kind of injuries?" I gasp.

"He is OK, but he's injured his right hip and also has some open wounds on his face." Mia is my calm antithesis.

"Which hospital?" I ask, looking at Corrin, who is looking back at me tenderly with concern.

"Trident Hospital, in North Charleston," Mia says. "They just left, so the ambulance should arrive there in about forty-five minutes."

As I lower my phone to the bar, it's all I can do at this moment to not lay my head down next to my phone and sob. I feel like a fool for thinking I could have a night off from the responsibilities running roughshod over my life.

TAKE RISKS AND LIVE IN THE MOMENT

Corrin is beyond kind, offering support and well wishes to Dad, also telling me she's here if there's anything she can do to help. While waiting for the check, I drink my wine down in one gulp before I walk out, feeling heavier with each step back into the hard times outside the noisy bar. It's like the weight of the world, the weight of Dad's entire life, is crushing my shoulders.

AUGUST 4, 2022

Dad is in Trident Hospital for a week, and the only blessing to this is that this hospital is only fifteen minutes from my home, compared to the hour drive I usually have to the VVH. Fifteen minutes becomes hours and hours inside the hospital, every single day, as Dad recovers as best he can from this nasty hip fracture. (Fun fact: Dad had hip replacement surgery on the other hip, the left one, a few years back.) Thankfully, this hip break doesn't require surgery, but it does require a month or two of healing. Dad's face also took several lacerations from his fall, leaving him with twenty-six staples.

He's in rough shape. Real rough. His tremendous pain is even crueler because he doesn't know why he hurts. Because of his dementia, he is confused, angry, and ornery, and you know what? I don't blame him. I would be too.

Dad has cursed out every nurse and doctor who has stepped foot into his room. I feebly try my best to calm him with bribes of KFC mashed potatoes, but not even the Colonel can help us now.

Finally back home (what a cruel use of this word) in his bed at the VVH, Dad now has a special mattress with "wings." The wings are mattress edges that surround Dad, almost hugging him, helping to keep him inside the bed, like a swaddled baby in a crib. "At least something is hugging him when I'm not around," I think.

He also has a giant pink Styrofoam block wedged between his legs to stabilize his hip. Try explaining to someone with dementia why there is a large block between their legs at all times. It's like the movie *Groundhog Day*, where you have infinite opportunities to piss off a man who can't remember your best attempts, leaving both parties frustrated over and over again.

If that isn't enough torture, Dad has to be moved by an actual machine, at least once a day, to a tall pleather wheelchair for physical therapy. With his injury, there's too much danger and liability for a nurse to move him. Rather than be touched by human hands, Dad is strapped into a basketlike cloth contraption that gently pulls him up into the air, like a kiddy ride at Chuck E. Cheese. Hoisted over his bed, he levitates until he's carefully lowered into the wheelchair. All this is controlled by a nurse, almost like controlling a drone. Only the drone is Dad flying from a bed to a wheelchair.

SEPTEMBER 7, 2022

Dad's hip recovery takes a full month, at the end of which, Mia, the head nurse on the Lyon's Unit, has hard news. Mia is my personal favorite, but it falls to her to tell me that Dad's doctor is recommending Dad go into hospice care.

We're out in the hall when Mia gives me this blow, and God bless her, she tries to do it as gently as possible, but there's just no way to receive that news gently. I'm confused as hell because Dad has pretty much recovered from the hip break and doesn't appear to be dying. Isn't hospice just special care for someone while they're dying?

Mia explains that Dad's weight loss led to a dangerously low body mass index (BMI). He is frailer than ever, his kidneys are failing, and he is rapidly declining neurologically. She explains that the doctor

TAKE RISKS AND LIVE IN THE MOMENT

does not believe he can get back to his baseline at this point and thinks that hospice care, right there at the VVH, will benefit Dad greatly because he will receive even more care and attention.

He doesn't have to move into another facility or even a new room. I stare at Mia blankly. Mia then explains that if Dad really does get better, he can come off hospice care. This eases my mind slightly, and I agree that whatever the doctor thinks is the right thing to do. Hospice care will start next week, and Mia says she'll monitor Dad closely, reporting every single detail to me every step of the way. I'm so grateful for Mia. I trust her.

After this hallway talk, we return to Dad's room, and I head to the right side of his bed and hold his hand. He hasn't been talking much today, and we've mostly been watching (a.k.a., staring) at the television. As soon as I sit in the chair by his bed and take his hand, he opens his mouth and says to me, "I don't want to die."

I'm shaken to my core, but I hold it together and tell Dad, "You're not going to die. You're going to get better." No amount of his dementia or my delusion can convince us that this is anything but a bald-faced lie.

NOVEMBER 10, 2022

Dad is getting so much more attention and care that he responds well to hospice care. The hospice team spoils him and gives him just about anything he asks for. He's about as happy as a man in this situation could be, and his anger has subsided from a raging boil to a simmer, which is a relief for everyone involved, especially me.

Lately Dad's been asking for egg salad sandwiches. On each visit, Dad recites a lengthy list of food requests, hoping I can bring them to him immediately. Last night I boiled a ton of eggs, found an egg salad recipe on Pinterest, and made cute little egg salad sandwiches for Dad and his roommate, Charlie.

Dylan isn't in Charleston right now, so we spent hours on the phone, chatting while I was making sammies for the elderly gentlemen. The phone conversation obviously ended in the ol' "You hang up; no, *you* hang up."

The next day is Veteran's Day, and I'm hanging with Dad and Charlie, telling them stories from my California trip with Dylan. Dad struggles to listen intently as he slowly chews his egg salad sandwich, but I notice him drifting after a few minutes.

Charlie is all about my stories and chimes in with several California stories of his own from his younger years. It seems strange that a stranger is more invested in this conversation than my father, but these are strange times in our lives.

I've also brought some art supplies and am making Veteran's Day cards for Dad, Charlie, and a few other residents I've had the pleasure of befriending these past several months.

During the breezy conversation between the three of us (OK, fine, it's mostly Charlie and I, but whatever), I hear a male voice start to scream. He seems to be in the room next to Dad and Charlie. The screaming man alternates between loud moans and screaming things like "Fuck youuuuuuuuuuu" and "Shittttttttttttt" at the top of his lungs.

Shocked, I put my hand over my mouth. Dad looks at me and calmly says, "That's the Screamer. He does this all the time."

I'm trying to ignore the screams from the room next door when Dad bursts out, "Squirt him!"

Then Charlie follows with "Kick him in the balls!"

I'm not sure whether to be appalled or to laugh. I choose laughter, as I most often do.

TAKE RISKS AND LIVE IN THE MOMENT

The Screamer, as well as Dad and Charlie, all stop screaming after a few moments, and everyone goes back to normal, as if nothing has happened.

When the guys have demolished the sandwiches and nothing's left on their paper plates but literal breadcrumbs, Charlie asks Dad if he would like some ice cream for dessert.

"Yes, of course," Dad answers, as if he couldn't believe the question even needed to be asked.

Charlie nods and turns his wheelchair to wheel himself into the hallway. I feel the need to mention that Charlie is blind, but this is a recent development, so he is running into furniture and walls as he wheels himself out of the room. Like Dad, Charlie has dementia.

After he has bumped his way into the hall, I hear Charlie yell at the top of his New York lungs, "Hey, we need two ice creams down here right away."

Charlie then maneuvers his wheelchair back into Dad's side of the room and stops at the entrance to proudly proclaim in his heavy accent, "The order has been placed." After a slight pause, Charlie adds, "With vigor," which sounds more like "viga." Then he turns his wheelchair and returns to his side of the room for the rest of the afternoon.

Charlie is successful; small vanilla ice cream cups are delivered to both sides of the room by a lovely nurse. With the curtains now drawn, Dad and I sit in silence. He is lying in his bed eating the ice cream with a plastic spoon while I wriggle in the same hard-ass chair in the corner I have yet to replace. I turn on Dad's television and find a music channel playing solid gold oldies.

As Four Tops belt out the lyrics of "Reach Out I'll Be There," I am grateful to have another visit with Dad more cognitively aware of his surroundings than not. These special moments seem fewer and farther between these days, and I'm keenly aware each moment like this one could be our last. There's just no way to know.

As if Dad is reading my mind, he looks at me, intensely, and tells me how proud he is of me. I'm blessed in this moment with an awareness of how important this conversation is, so I grab my cell phone and hit record. I capture every word that comes out of Dad's mouth. I want to document this because I know I may never hear him so lucid again.

Dad tells me what a great accomplishment it is for a father to see his daughter rise to every experience they are faced with in life, good or bad. He tells me that he appreciates how close we've been my whole life. He says that he has always told me I'd be in the publishing business and that I would be a writer and now I am ("But I'm not," I think). He says that he is just so proud of all my accomplishments and all the people I've helped in my life, also saying he knows I will help many more people in my lifetime.

The oldies play in the background while Dad tells me all these amazing things, and my eyes fill with tears. The moment sinks in, and yet again I feel like I'm in a movie. It feels like my life has been full of these movie moments since Dad left his home for the last time.

I relish this moment with Dad until it's time for me to head home for the night. I gather my belongings, kiss Dad on the cheek, and tell him I'll see him next weekend. I call out, "I love you" as I walk out of his room and stop at the bulletin board to hang the Veteran's Day cards that I've made for Dad and Charlie. I drop the others at the front desk and continue on to my other life, the one in Charleston that I have so little energy left to live.

TAKE RISKS AND LIVE IN THE MOMENT

WEDNESDAY, NOVEMBER 16, 2022, 8:00 A.M.

In my kitchen as I'm groggily starting the coffee, my phone starts to ring, and I look at the screen. I'm not shocked that it's the VVH. I answer the phone while also thinking about what I'm going to wear to the office today.

"Hi, Jaclyn," Mia says, "How are you?"

I'm instantly aware that her tone is off, almost sad. Why is she asking how I am? She never asks how I am. Don't get me wrong. I adore Mia, and we have a great relationship, but calls from her are short and matter of fact—straight to business.

"Um … I'm fine," I say with suspicion in my voice and then, "What's up, Mia?"

Mia proceeds to tell me that Dad had an "incident" this morning. During this incident, he was in a tremendous amount of pain, but he could not vocalize anything. She says that he was thrashing in his bed and screaming, so they had to give him a lot of morphine and Ativan to calm him down.

Then Mia says she believes that Dad is "transitioning and actively dying" and that I need to get up there to the VVH as soon as possible, and I need to tell my brother to do the same.

What the hell is she talking about? I was just with Dad a few days ago, and we had the best conversation we've had all year. He was doing pretty great, all things considered!

"Mia, have you called the right person?" I ask her, not believing anything she is saying can possibly be true and quite frankly doubting her sanity at this moment. "This is Jaclyn, Shelby's daughter; you've obviously called the wrong person."

"I'm so sorry, Jaclyn. I've called the right person," Mia responds. "I know this seems sudden and is extremely difficult, but we truly believe that your dad is actively dying right now."

"I'll be there in an hour. Thank you, Mia," I say, confused. I watch my hand put the phone down on the kitchen counter but feel as if it is not actually attached to my body. It's like I'm watching someone else's hand set down my phone. I am so numb.

Five minutes later I'm in my car, on the way to Walterboro, in utter disbelief that this is actually happening. Dad is "actively dying." This is a phrase I've never heard before, much like the term *transitioning*. It's all so foreign and wrong.

At a stoplight, I dial Corinne's number. She picks up right away, and I regurgitate everything Mia told me but insist I don't believe this is true. There has to be a mistake, but I'm driving up there anyway, just to see what the hell is going on with Dad.

Corinne offers to drive from Atlanta to Walterboro to be with me, but I tell her no. I tell her to stay put because I honestly don't think this is really happening. Corinne sounds uncertain of my certainty, but she agrees to wait for my update.

I call Lance to inform him and my sister-in-law, Laura, of the situation. They are both concerned and tell me to update them as soon as I better understand what is going on.

"This is fine; everything is fine," I say to myself over and over again on the drive. Mia obviously made a mistake, and we'll all laugh about this later. Still, VVH is definitely going to owe me some flowers or something for this scare.

WEDNESDAY, NOVEMBER 16, 2022, 9:15 A.M.

After signing in at the front desk for the millionth time, I walk down the main hall, past my bird friends, who are not early and won't be getting any worms. "Sleeping in?" I thought. "How nice for them."

TAKE RISKS AND LIVE IN THE MOMENT

My magical thinking tells me that everything must be OK for my birds to have taken the morning off.

When I finally get to Dad's room, I am not prepared. Dad looks completely wrong. His skin is pale and yellowish. He's lying in his bed on his back with his knees bent, covered by a white sheet and blue blanket. The shape of his legs from under the blanket is shocking; his legs are indescribably thin. Dad's rib cage pokes out through the soft maroon cotton golf shirt I recently purchased from Goodwill. His face is gaunt, cheeks sunken, and his mouth is barely open.

All my bargaining and illusions collapse in the shadow of Dad's architecture of bones pressing up through his sickly skin. Everything Mia told me on the phone was accurate. Dad is dying.

Holy shit, Dad is dying. Actively. Dying.

A hospice nurse sits next to Dad. She stands up and introduces herself to me. She is Nancy. Nancy then instructs me to sit down in her vacated chair.

"I've been sitting with him all morning so that he wouldn't be alone," Nancy says sweetly. "I'll be here with you, as much or as little as you need, until he transitions."

There's that word again.

Nancy reaches into her leather workbag to retrieve a pamphlet titled *Gone from My Sight, the Dying Experience.*

I take the pamphlet, and again my hand feels like a prop, the possession of some other woman. Truth be told, my entire body feels like it belongs to someone else. Nothing feels real. This is the worst movie I've ever seen.

Nancy talks about things I can expect to happen over the next twenty-four hours, and she keeps asking if I understand. I nod each time, pretending that I do. But I can't understand anything that is happening right now.

Mia enters Dad's room, approaches my chair, bends down, and hugs me. "I'm so sorry," she says. This is when I start crying.

I slip out of the room to call Lance and Laura and tell them that it's true. Dad is "actively dying."

Lance tells me he's leaving his home in Atlanta now and will be here in a few hours. Laura tells me how sorry she is. Everyone is sorry, but nobody is as sorry as I am.

I call Sara, crying hysterically. She's already on her way to Walterboro. Corinne called her after we spoke, and they decided, no matter what the outcome was going to be, Sara would come since she was the closest. Now we know what the outcome is going to be. I am about to lose my dad. I have been motherless for seven years, and I am about to be fatherless too. The rest of my life I will be an orphan, and it doesn't matter how old you are when that happens—it's always too soon.

I sit vigil with Dad as staff wander in and out of the room, checking on Dad, and me. Everyone is so unbelievably kind, offering me beverages and food. They offer anything to help me feel more comfortable. I'm thankful, but I don't want anything. I just want to rewind my life a couple of decades, back to a time when Mom was alive and she and Dad were thriving, and we were a happy family, and I felt safe.

Sara arrives, and the hours slip by. She occupies a new chair in Dad's room. They have countless chairs for anyone who will help me through this nightmare.

Sara has brought a bag of my favorite snacks and tells me that Corinne and Kim are on their way, but Lisa had to stay behind because of work. Of course, they're on their way. These women … my tribe … my family … my sisters—I love them with all my heart.

As I look at Sara, sitting in the room with Dad, something dawns on me. "It was you," I say to Sara.

TAKE RISKS AND LIVE IN THE MOMENT

"What do you mean, it was me? What was me?" Sara asks, confused.

"You called here and asked them to have Dad call me on my birthday, didn't you?" I ask, knowing without a doubt I'm right.

Sara nods her head. I tell her how much I love her for that, for everything.

"Is Dylan coming?" Sara asks me.

"No, I don't want him to have to go through this," I say.

The reason I do not want him to go through this is because just a year ago, he lost the love of his life to cancer. Dylan was with her as she "transitioned." I don't want him to relive that with me. Honestly, I don't know if we are even at that point in our relationship, and it feels a little too soon to pull him into this intimate situation.

Lance arrives, and another chair is dragged into Dad's room. We form an audience, watching Dad's active dying. Dad has been nonverbal since I arrived hours before. He's on so much morphine and Ativan for his pain and to help him "transition peacefully." I wonder if it would be inappropriate for me to ask for some drugs to help me with my pain at his transition.

I break the deafening silence in the room by talking to Dad. I take his hand in mine, and I ask him if he knows that we are here with him.

Though the man has not uttered a word all day and I'm unsure he even speaks, I swear he answers me, whispering, "Yeah." I swear he does. Lance hears it. I start to cry again. This time the sorrowful tears running down my face are mixed with happiness and relief. I'm so happy he knows we're here with him. I'm relieved that he is not alone, but I'm so damn sad that this is happening. I'm losing the most important man in my life.

Corinne and Kim arrive, and I go to the front desk to meet them. I hug each of them so tightly I might break them. Kim decides to hang back in the large atrium area, just down the hall from Dad's room. She lost her own dad a few months ago, and it's just too fresh. She can't endure seeing my dad like this. Of course, I understand. It's more than enough that she came.

Corinne comes back to Dad's room, sits in the chair beside Dad, and talks to him for a few minutes. They've always had such a special relationship. Corinne, being her positive, funny self, recounts to Dad humorous memories they've shared over the years. One of our favorites involves the odd little peanuts Dad gifted her weekly as a kid, and the fact that he brought an eight-foot, handmade Mr. Peanut to her wedding, monocle and all. I bet he's laughing inside. She then leans down and whispers something to Dad.

Later she'll tell me what she said: "You can let go now, Shelby. We've got Jaclyn."

By 10:00 p.m., Nancy explains that Dad probably has another twenty-four to forty-eight hours left before he fully "transitions." Nancy's been there all day, and she's a true godsend. She encourages us to go home for the evening. But I can't. Out of concern for my dad, I ask Mia if they can make an exception and allow me to sleep in Dad's room with him.

The next thing I know, a couple of maintenance men wheel a fancy-looking cot into the corner of Dad's room, and they even place a mattress pad on top of it for extra comfort. I am staggered by their kindness. I may be exhausted beyond recognition and about to sleep on the flimsiest cot imaginable, but I know this is the right thing to do. I'll live to fight another day, but Dad has two at most.

TAKE RISKS AND LIVE IN THE MOMENT

THURSDAY, NOVEMBER 17, 2022, 6:00 A.M.

I'm back in the chair next to Dad, holding his hand. I couldn't sleep at all last night, so I rolled out of bed before dawn and moved to that damned wooden chair, next to Dad. The thought of Dad dying without me right beside him is too much to bear. He's been there by my side for my entire life, in good and bad times, and now it's my turn.

Dad's completely out of it, practically unconscious, but I talk to him like he can hear me. You never know, right? I talk about our trip to Disney World and the stuffed Dumbo he got me when I was kid. I tell him how much the Signs of Spring walks meant to me and that I'll continue looking for signs of spring for the rest of my life. I tell him that I will think of him every time I see a little bud sprouting out of the ground after a long, cold winter.

Dad's room is located almost at the very end of the hall, by the exit doors, which are always locked to prevent the vets from going AWOL. Here at the end of the hall, a distraught man is trying to open the locked doors. He screams at the nurses who come down the hall. He tells them he has a job to get to and a truck to unload, and they'll be sorry if they don't help him get out of here and get to work. My already broken heart crumbles to dust as I listen to him.

When the screaming finally becomes too much for me, I step out into the hall and lock eyes with a bouncy nurse named Brenda. She tells me, "He's a new guy, and he's confused, looking for his wife."

That statement hits me right in the gut, and I feel my stomach turn. This poor man. I can't imagine how scared and lost he must feel right now. Everything he knows is gone, and he has no idea where he is and why he can't leave. He's literally locked inside this strange place. I hope he doesn't realize how strongly it always smells like pee.

Nursing home staff members come in and out of Dad's room to hug him, and me. They come to say their goodbyes to Dad, which is gut wrenching. They love him, and they've never even seen him at his best.

A lady I don't know enters Dad's room and asks if I'm his daughter. I tell her that I am indeed his daughter, extending my hand to shake hers. She bypasses my hand and hugs me hard.

Then she says, "Your father is so proud of you. I'm a nurse's assistant here, and I'd sit with him sometimes in the evenings, and all he talks about is you. He's so proud that you're a published author, and he just goes on and on about how talented you are … about what a gift you have."

She proceeds to ask me for the name of the book I recently published because she promised Dad she would read it. Shocked, I barely have the heart to tell the woman that I am not a writer.

Reluctantly, I confess that I work for a publishing company, but I, myself, am not a published author. I'm in human resources, not the creative side of the publishing house. She's surprised; Dad was so emphatic and believable. We share a cute little chuckle about it, chalking the whole thing up to Dad's dementia, though she keeps saying how real it seemed.

Somehow Dad knew that my employer would share his vision and bring me into the creative side with this amazing opportunity to share our story. Who knew that working for this publishing company and seeing Dad through this saga would one day result in this book? I guess Dad did.

TAKE RISKS AND LIVE IN THE MOMENT

THURSDAY, NOVEMBER 17, 2022, 10:45 A.M.

Midmorning, a hospice nurse enters Dad's room to tell me she needs forty-five minutes to give Dad a sponge bath. Lance is here by this point, and we walk into the hall to give them privacy. I'm relieved someone is up for the task of bathing Dad. I suppose he wants to exit this world clean. I think I would. Strange how they clean new babies and the dying in the same manner, with a sponge.

In the hall, Lance and I are greeted by a tall, beautiful African American woman. She introduces herself as the hospice chaplain, Maeve. She radiates such kindness and grace that I feel calmer just being in her presence. Maeve tells us that she visited Dad several times the past couple of weeks, most recently two days ago. She assured us that Dad has a strong relationship with God, and she's confident he will "transition" peacefully. Maeve's soothing voice pierces my strained vigilance and ushers in space for me to breathe.

Maeve then pulls a small notebook out of her purse, along with a pen, and asks us what our plans are for Dad's final arrangements.

I tell her that Dad wants to be buried with Mom at Fort Lincoln Cemetery in Maryland, just outside Washington, DC. He already put his name on Mom's headstone so they can be together eternally. However, I must confess that Lance and I are unsure whether Dad's body will be buried or cremated. This has been a huge discussion the past few months.

Dad does not want to be cremated; he wants to be buried. However, he is not leaving any money behind, and burial is more than twice as expensive as cremation. We only have a couple thousand dollars left from the estate sale, and Lance thinks we need to make the financially responsible decision. Every time we discuss it, my eyes well up with tears. My brain knows Lance's point is valid, but my heart is unsure. Burial is our father's last wish, and I don't know if I can go against it. It's the man's final wish, for God's sake.

Trying to hold back my tears, I tell Maeve all of this. She offers us the sweetest smile I've ever seen and says, "Oh honey, your father knows the Lord, and it doesn't matter what happens to the shell that is his body. He is going to be with God. Cremate that wonderful man."

I'm so relieved to hear her words that I lean over and embrace Maeve. She has freed my heart, and I thank her for giving me permission to cremate Dad. Lance looks relieved too. I mean, if a woman of God gave us permission, it's cool, right?

We chat a little longer, and Maeve tells us that we need to "release" Dad, which means telling him aloud that we are releasing him. She says that this is important because Dad could be hanging on just for us.

Maeve also encourages us to open a window, which seems very woo-woo and super bizarre to me. But if this angelic human tells me to do something, I'm going to do it. She shares that it is believed an open window in the room of the dying allows the souls of deceased family members to enter and escort the person into the next life together.

Lance leaves me with Maeve while he spends a few minutes alone with Dad.

I pace up and down the hall, thankful that the new guy has calmed down and is in his room.

When Lance comes back to the hall, it's my turn to go in and "release" Dad. I tiptoe into Dad's room, scared to death of the conversation I'm supposed to have with the man I love the most. I walk to the window and open it up about an inch. It's freaking freezing outside, and it seems cruel to let Dad be uncomfortable in his final moments. Also, the dead can fit through an inch of window, right?

I sit in the chair next to Dad and put his hand in mine. I say, "Dad, I'm going to be OK, I promise. I want you to go be with Mom. I release you."

Then, with the tears streaming down my cheeks, I slowly recite the Lord's Prayer, his favorite. He squeezes my hand ever so delicately, a miraculous feat for a man straddling two worlds with more of him in the next one than the one we share. I cannot help but cry, though I do it as quietly as possible, so Dad doesn't think I'm rescinding his release. Then, I pick up my phone and play one of Dad's favorite songs, "Fly Me to the Moon," sung by Frank Sinatra.

FRIDAY, NOVEMBER 18, 2022

For a few hours that day, the longest Friday of my life, Lance stays with Dad while Corinne and Kim get me out for a little while. They drive me home to Charleston, to my house, though I am scared to death, literally and figuratively, to leave Dad. Still, I shower and put on clean clothes. I love on my kitties for a few minutes, which warms my heart and soothes my soul. A shower and cat contact are exactly what I need to give me the strength to return to my vigil.

When we return to the nursing home, I find that something has changed. Not with Dad but with me. Stepping away from this intense and grueling situation has made it nearly impossible to return. In the white space of a little distance, the full horror of this picture was in full effect. Even a small reprieve from the horror has made the reality that I am watching Dad die all the more horrifying. I don't know if I can bear it or how I might. But with no choice, I sit by Dad and cry for hours.

After my breakdown, Corinne and Lance come to be with me in Dad's room. They are worried about me. The three of us sit quietly together, peacefully waiting there with Dad.

That night, I lean close to Dad and speak to him, and I know he hears me. Well, I don't know, but I choose to believe he does. When I speak, he moves his face and his eyes a bit and makes a few unintelligible sounds, like he is trying to talk. It's so bittersweet, feeling utterly loved, knowing that he is trying to talk to me, yet heartbroken by the guttural sounds that he can manage and his inability to speak.

I'm shattered. Lance asks Corinne and me if we are up for pizza for dinner. As Lance steps away to call it in, pulling back the curtain of Dad's room and entering the common area Dad shares with his new roommate, Stan (Charlie was moved to another room), Corinne and I hear the loudest fart we have ever heard. I'm telling you; it shakes the room.

A few seconds later, Lance pulls the curtain back and walks back into Dad's room, sheepishly saying, "I just need to make it perfectly clear that that was not me." Corinne and I fall into fits of hysterical laughter, like we are kids again, and, God, do I need that laughing fit.

An hour later, Corinne, Kim, Lance, and I sit in the atrium eating Papa John's pizza. We laugh about Stan's fart and other funny things that happened the past couple of days. It's a nice moment. It feels like family, and I no longer feel alone.

After dinner, I return to Dad's room, casually glancing into Stan's room, because his curtain is open. Stan is usually in a wheelchair, but now he is kneeling on the floor, against his bed, naked from the waist down. I try to avert my eyes but am mesmerized by Stan's gyrations. As he rocks back and forth, back and forth, over and over again, it appears that he is trying to have sexual relations with his bed.

When I am able to tear my horrified gaze away, I turn and walk back down the hall, to the nurse's station, where I tell them I think that Stan needs some assistance, raising my eyebrows to let them know something is afoot.

Late that night, I am lying on the cot in the corner of Dad's room once again and trying to drift off to sleep, but the alarm on Stan's bed notifying the nurses that he's out of bed keeps going off. I'm concerned for Stan but also, I'm not going to lie, I'm a little concerned for myself. It's not every day Stan has a woman in his room, and he seems to have been a little randy earlier. I text Corinne, telling her about the situation and that I am a little scared for my safety. Corinne's reply is simple: "I don't care if he's elderly or not, sweep the leg!"

I lie back down, futilely trying to ignore the bed alarm. Then I hear Stan's nurse enter the room and quietly say, "Sweetie, you can't keep getting on your knees to say your prayers. God will accept your prayers even if you say them in your bed." I guess Stan's naked piety confused me.

SATURDAY, NOVEMBER 19, 2022

For days I've stayed in Dad's room, refusing to risk the slightest chance he could die all by himself. These grinding cycles of grief, absurdity, and yes, laughs have taken their toll on me, and by the time Saturday arrives, I am exhausted, running on fumes. He has been so quiet, so still, barely making any sounds at all. Friday he made uncomfortable breathing sounds that were terrifying to listen to. Nancy described them as "terminal secretions." I don't like my new vocabulary. I wish I wasn't taking this class in the language of dying.

By Saturday somehow Corinne and Kim are actually able to convince me to go back to the Holiday Inn with them to sleep for a few hours. Nancy helps by again promising to notify me of the slightest change in Dad's condition. The three of us share a bottle of red wine and drink out of plastic Holiday Inn cups. I tell them how much I love them and that I can't even think of ever doing life without them. And that I'm forever grateful that they are here for me right now, in one of my most difficult life experiences.

As we chat, I flip through the journal I've been keeping since Dad was first hospitalized almost a year ago. (Come on, how else do you think I would have remembered all this?) I smile, looking over the pages of the journal, which are adorned with every single VVH visitor sticker I've collected over the past seven months, even the one Dylan wore the day he came with me and met Dad.

I have no idea why I've insisted on collecting each one of these, but they make me proud and happy for some reason. They are a tangible record of one of the worst years of my life, but also proof of the precious time I was able to spend with Dad. I look at the very back page and see that there is only room for one more sticker. I gasp. Dad is dying tomorrow, I think to myself.

SUNDAY, NOVEMBER 20, 2022

Nancy has been in and out of Dad's room with me all day, and I feel like she's a family member at this point. I can't imagine going through this without her, especially since Corinne and Lance both left this morning. Corinne has an event with her daughter back in Atlanta that she cannot miss, though she felt awful leaving me.

I'm unsure why Lance left—maybe because Dad's dying has taken a lot longer than anyone expected, or he just needed or wanted to get home to his family. But Kim, sweet Kim, has stayed behind as the sacrificial lamb to my grief, though she still can't go into Dad's room, which I also understand. Bless her unfailingly loyal heart: just a text message away if I need her, she sits all day in the atrium.

So much sitting. Endless sitting. I watch Dad breathe. I wonder when I'm going to lose him for good. Dad's breathing is more rapid now, and Nancy describes it as "accessory breathing." For two more hours, I play Frank Sinatra for Dad from my phone.

Around three, I start to lose it a little, wondering how much longer we will wait. Then I instantly feel guilty about wondering. I shouldn't want this to speed up. I should want this to slow down. I'm just so tired.

I text Kim that we should leave the nursing home for a late lunch. I need to get out of here. She is on board, and we meet at the front of the home. I pop one of the Nicorette lozenges I've been feverishly chewing lately (I finally quit vaping because Dylan was grossed out by it, and frankly, I was too), and Kim and I head to a nearby bar we find on Google, because this mama needs a stiff drink.

We slink into the deep wooden booths of the hole-in-the-wall bar, located within a mile of the nursing home. It's dark, which is perfect. I order a vodka soda, and Kim orders a beer. We glance at the menu and order a couple of sandwiches.

I'm not much of a conversationalist today, but Kim doesn't care. She's just there. Like she always is. By my side. I order a second vodka soda and pick at my food. The waitress is overly friendly and chatty. Every time she comes to the table, I die a little inside, wishing she would keep her sunny disposition to herself and just leave us alone in the dark.

When Kim has almost finished her turkey sandwich, something hits me. I feel an overwhelming sense of urgency, and I know, in my heart, that Dad is about to die. I tell Kim we have to leave right now, and she is up before I even finish the sentence, looking for the waitress to pay.

I run into Dad's room, and Nancy is there, telling me things have just started to decline. Dad's breathing is now very shallow as I watch the breaths slowly rise and fall from his frail body. Nancy listens to Dad's heart through her stethoscope and tells me his heartbeat is irregular now, which is what happens shortly before someone "transitions."

Holy shit, this is it. God, why didn't I pay closer attention to the damn death pamphlet they gave me days ago? I would know what is about to happen if I had!

I sit with Dad for another couple of hours, frozen in fear. Nancy returns and puts her fingers to Dad's left wrist. She softly tells me that she can no longer detect a pulse. She says this is normal and everything is OK. His pulse is just too faint to detect at this point.

I try to remain calm, and Nancy tells me to talk to Dad, but I don't know what to say. I try to remember stories about my childhood that he would like. I say, "Dad, do you remember when you used to brush my hair when I was a little girl, and it became such a pain that you cut my hair short?"

"Dad, remember when you coached Corinne's and my softball team?"

"Dad, remember when you and Mom and I would go on road trips when I was little, and you'd make me listen to Neil Diamond the whole time?"

"I'll never ever forget those Signs of Spring walks, Dad. Never."

I hold Dad's hand gently like he held my hand on our walks and watch him struggling to breathe. It's brutal. I'm not sure I'm going to survive this. Nancy counts Dad's breaths per minute; he's down to three breaths per minute—it's that labored.

I grab my phone and put on "My Way" by Frank Sinatra. Mom left this world listening to her favorite band, the Rolling Stones, and Dad would have his favorite playing too.

Just after seven-thirty, I hold on to Dad's hand, trying not to be scared, but I am. God, I am. This isn't about me, though. This is about him. I will not act scared. I will be calm as I walk him out of this life. "Go be with Mom," I quietly whisper. Then he takes his last breath.

BE CONFIDENT IN YOUR CHOICES

Confidence in your choices shows your commitment to your character and the scene. When you fully commit to your character's choices and convictions, you strengthen the scene and make your character more believable and compelling.

After my graduation from Georgia Southern University, the writing was on the wall—my college internship would not result in a permanent job. My dream job as a child life specialist (working with hospitalized children) at the Medical Center of Central Georgia, or anywhere else, required a master's degree. The dream remained a fantasy because there was no way I would return to college so soon after graduation. An advanced degree remained a "someday maybe" idea that never fell together.

Instead, I occupied a tiny apartment in Macon, Georgia, with my brand-new degree framed in a huge navy-blue frame (thanks, Dad) over my bedroom desk. I stared at the wall and wondered what the hell I was supposed to do. Was my degree forevermore just a pricey piece of home decor? My part-time job as a server at the Player's Club Restaurant graduated with me to a full-time gig until I figured out my next steps.

One Friday night while I was waiting tables, kismet intervened. Just before closing I helped a stranger find a lost piece of jewelry, and you'd think I'd found her lost child, not a charm bracelet. By chance or by design, she was the director of the Bibb County Department of Family and Children's Services and soon to be my boss at my first grown-up job.

Two weeks later I began my social work career. I was issued a desktop computer, pager (it was the early 2000s), desk phone, and cubicle so small that my giant framed degree consumed the entire space.

As a caseworker for Child Protective Services, I created treatment plans in substantiated cases of abuse or neglect. When children were removed from the home and placed in foster care, I established steps with each family to create and sustain a safe living environment, and then I monitored that family for a given amount of time, in hopes that the children returned home.

I enjoyed connecting with people and helping them. I loved the kids and felt like I was really making a difference, like a useful and productive member of society. I felt like a real adult.

Then a call from Dad one night left me feeling like a little girl. He told me Mom had experienced a serious incident earlier that day, as a result of uncontrolled blood sugar. She had not been following her diet as recommended and was inconsistent with her insulin. Some days Mom was not taking her insulin at all.

Today was one of those days, and her blood sugar had dropped really low, causing her to become unresponsive and nearly unconscious. Thankfully Dad was there when this occurred, and he was able

BE CONFIDENT IN YOUR CHOICES

to get some sugar into her system before she slipped into a diabetic coma. Dad told me that events like this had started happening fairly often recently, though today was the worst it had been.

I didn't understand how Mom could not do what she was supposed to do when it came to her diabetes. Why couldn't she honor her insulin schedule? Why couldn't she eat healthy? Why was she still eating junk food and ice cream like she was a teenager? The only real concession she seemed to honor since being diagnosed was switching from regular Coca-Cola to Diet. While this was actually a pretty big deal for her and I knew all this was hard on Mom, it was hard on Dad and me too.

It was made harder being so far away from the two people I loved the most, unable to support her and help her do better. I was building my career helping families make better and healthier choices, but I couldn't help my own family.

. . .

It was a sweltering June day when I rolled into Charleston, South Carolina, and the apartment Lisa and I were renting for the next year. I had given up my career in my early twenties like some women did to have babies, but I did it to care for my aging parents. Charleston seemed like the perfect place because it was less than two hours from Myrtle Beach, and in my opinion a much cooler town for a recent college graduate than Myrtle Beach, where my parents were surrounded by fellow retirees.

Lisa had tended bar and waited tables for a restaurant group in Atlanta part time for years, and they were about to open a restaurant in Charleston, so the timing was perfect for us both. We shared a two-bedroom apartment right outside Charleston. Then we had the time of our lives for the next year while Lisa and I helped open up a new restaurant that summer and became part of the waitstaff.

When we first moved in, Mom and Dad were right there to help, of course. They were excited to help set up my first official postcollege apartment, especially since they'd known Lisa for years. They arrived the day after Lisa and I moved in, and Dad, in full Martha Stewart mode, demanded that we each choose personalized colors for our bedrooms and said he would help us paint. We embarked to Sherwin-Williams, where I selected a mauve color named "Dressy Rose" and Lisa chose a shade of blue called "Moonmist." We were ready to splash sophistication all over the walls of our new home, but first we needed food.

We decided on a quick lunch at Wendy's before we got started painting. We took our places in a long line to the register. We were all nervous about this because Dad was terrible at waiting. He always said, "Jaclyn, I was on an aircraft carrier called the *Kitty Hawk* when I was in the navy, and I had to stand in the longest line you could ever imagine every single day, for four years, to get every one of my meals. I'll be damned if I will wait in line for my meals now."

I eyed Dad with trepidation, praying he would not make a scene about waiting in line. He stood with us for a few minutes, better behaved than I expected. Then he excused himself to go to the restroom. He was gone for about ten minutes, and by the time he reappeared, we were at the register, placing our order—perfect timing!

Relieved Dad missed the bulk of the wait time so there wouldn't be a scene, I relaxed for only a moment before I caught a dangerous glimmer in his eyes. Immediately, I recognized his annoyance tinged with anger. Oh god, what could have possibly happened in that restroom?

Dad slowly approached us at the register and did not utter a single word. Instead, he reached across the counter, past the Wendy's employee manning the register, and grabbed a sheet of wax paper right off the top that had been sitting in wait for food. He then proceeded to dramatically wipe his hands, which I then realized were wet, with the wax paper, very slowly, emphasizing every single wipe. Like a slow clap, all drama and exaggeration.

When he was done performatively drying his hands, he crumbled the damp paper liner into a ball and placed it back on the tray. Then he announced to every person in the Wendy's, "There are no paper towels in the men's room."

After a brief pause, maybe he expected applause for his performance, he added, "I'll have a number one with cheese, please."

Mom, Lisa, and I ate our food in silent embarrassment. Embarrassing scenes in public places were nothing new for Dad, but they became more frequent and almost unexpected as he aged.

Dad was completely oblivious or just unconcerned with our embarrassment. He felt no shame about making a scene and doubled down, always making sure to tell us and anyone within earshot, "Mark my words. This is most certainly the beginning of the demise of the customer service industry. We keep seeing these things everywhere. They were just talking about this sort of thing on Fox News last week."

...

The closest bar to our apartment was called the Village Tavern, and it was a real dive. This made me, Lisa, and our new friend Renee (our coworker and first official friend in Charleston), love it all the more. The bar was about a half mile away from our apartment, so we could easily walk/stagger home and retrieve any cars left behind in the morning.

Village Tavern offered no bells or whistles, just good food, good drinks, and good people. The three of us would saddle up to the bar after a long night of waiting tables at Queen Anne's Revenge, the pirate-themed restaurant full of bells and whistles where we all worked. At the homey tavern, we drank canned beer and took shots, sometimes until the sun came up.

We took turns spinning a huge shot wheel on the tavern wall to see what kind of shot we'd be taking. When left to our own devices, Jägerbombs were the shot of choice. The tavern was a live music venue for underground Indie music. We saw some amazing and emerging bands there, but we also saw some loud "garage bands" that were nothing but loud and should have stayed in their garages.

The main bartender at the Village Tavern was a shy recent college graduate with long brown hair. Sara was more reserved than we were, but it was obvious she enjoyed her fellow service workers, who never failed to tip generously. She named the three of us the "Queen Anne's Girls."

Sara's parents owned the tavern, and her brother was the general manager. Sara was from Charleston and was, like us, bartending until she figured out her next move. Sara slowly warmed up to us, and by the end of the summer, we were all thick as thieves, hanging out late after the bar closed, at the bar or back at the apartment Lisa and I shared.

Sara eventually assimilated with my best friends, my Marietta girls. This was a big deal, as a new girl had never been introduced to our hometown crew. Sara was special, though, and she just fit right in. Sara didn't just become a member of our group of girls; she helped solidify our group. She was the missing piece to our puzzle who completed the picture.

BE CONFIDENT IN YOUR CHOICES

A couple of years after Sara joined the group, we were on a group excursion, walking back to our hotel after a night of fabulous New York City debauchery. Arm in arm, Sara stopped us and suggested we give ourselves an official name. After looking around at these beautiful human beings who were everything to me, I glanced up at the awning just ahead of us, which read *McGee's Bar*.

"McGee's," I declared. "We should be the "McGees." Unanimous agreement followed as we crammed ourselves into a New York City cab.

We spent the entire cab ride laughing hysterically as we channeled our inner Spice Girls, selecting unique first names for each member of the McGees. Corinne was Classy McGee, always so put together, no matter the occasion. Like my mom, Corinne was never caught without her lipstick and matching gloss topcoat.

Poor Lisa ended up with Stinky McGee due to the fact that she'd recently gone on a trip with her boyfriend, who jokingly wrote "Stinky" on her luggage tag without her knowing. We thought this was the funniest story we'd ever heard, and it just had to be her McGee name. Kim became Shorty McGee because, well, she's short. Sara was Poppy McGee because she loved all things pop culture.

I was and will forevermore be known as Wheezie McGee because when I get to laughing really hard, I wheeze. Our sixth and final McGee was Philip, Corinne's serious boyfriend, who was on that trip with us and whom she would later marry. Philip was an honorary McGee because he felt like he belonged with us girls and we gave him the nickname of Wacky McGee.

In Charleston, I waited tables with Lisa, having the best time living a carefree life without a "real job." But deep down I longed for more, something meaningful, and soon landed back on the social work horse at the Berkeley County Department of Social Services.

This time I investigated suspected abuse or neglect and I was the one who placed the kids in foster care. Over two and a half years, I separated several children from their parents to be placed in foster care. Half my days were spent interviewing children at their schools and homes, identifying horrific warning signs. I never took a child from a home unless there was a good reason, but still it hurt each time.

I also worried about my own safety. Social workers have been killed by angry parents. The fact that I was a twenty-something blonde flanked by cops didn't help. The things I saw and the threats I received could fill a second book.

• • •

I stayed in social work a few more years until I burned out under the stress. I was almost thirty years old and just not feeling right. Recurring headaches started plaguing me, and I struggled to sleep. My new primary care doctor, Dr. Kinney, diagnosed me with high blood pressure, exacerbated by stress, and put me on blood pressure meds.

"But I'm not even thirty years old yet; I don't want to be on blood pressure meds!" I whined to Dr. Kinney.

She quickly responded, "Then you may want to think about a new job. Or figure out how you can better handle your stress."

Ha! If she only knew that I've been trying to figure that out since I was a kid.

I tried customer service, bill collecting (I know, I know), pharmaceutical research, and finally planted myself into a midsize local technology company.

The company was known around town as being a fun place to work, and it was big enough for me to try out different career paths internally. I started as an account manager and later trained customers all over the country on how to use our cutting-edge software.

BE CONFIDENT IN YOUR CHOICES

That role was a dream come true for a couple of years, until I found the position of all positions: culture coordinator on the culture team. They had a team dedicated to company culture! Can you imagine? I hit the jackpot! There I was, culture coordinator of this big ol' technology company, whose job was to help foster a positive work environment and ensure that our employees were as happy as possible. I was living the dream!

But then came the nightmare.

The call was from the same Myrtle Beach emergency room that would call when Dad was discovered unconscious years later. Dad's situation was the sequel.

Mom's ER visit was not a giant surprise, but it was still upsetting. Her health had declined rapidly in recent years as her diabetes took a toll on her entire body. The diabetes had led to a massive heart attack several years prior to this ER visit. She'd had quadruple bypass heart surgery in her late fifties, and she'd somehow survived it like a champ, but it didn't keep her on track after she returned home.

Her uncontrolled diabetes resulted in neuropathy, which caused major numbness and weakness in her legs and feet. The neuropathy left her wobbly and unstable at best and barely able to walk at worst. She had to use a walker at all times, and we were all trying to accept the situation and be as positive as possible. It was tough, and it got tougher. What we never saw coming and were not remotely prepared for was her dementia. Mom was only sixty-five when we began to see the terrifying signs of what we'd later learn was Lewy body dementia (LBD), a disease that creates abnormal deposits of protein in the brain. LBD leads to problems with thinking, moving, mood, and behavior, exacerbating her difficulty caring for herself with diabetes.

I cannot explain how devastating it is to watch your parent lose her mind … oh wait, I just did. Lucky me, turns out *both* of my parents would develop dementia. Mom had good days and bad days, but nights were the worst. She often called me in the middle of the night, crying because a man had broken into her home and was holding her hostage. That man was Dad. Sometimes she had no idea who he was, even though he was her devoted caregiver. She also often forgot to use her walker when walking to or from the bathroom, which is how she ended up falling and breaking her hip.

Of course, when I received the ER call, I ran out of my office building and drove straight to Myrtle Beach, not even stopping to pack a bag. I was still a hospital rookie. Though she'd survived quadruple bypass in the past, by the time she broke her hip, she was a very different woman. Mom barely made it through hip replacement surgery. After that struggle, she was discharged to a shitty little rehab facility, where she got sicker.

For a week, I desperately tried to have her moved to a better facility, only to have her returned to the ER for severe pneumonia. At Mom's side around the clock in the intensive care unit, Dad and I spent two weeks hoping and praying for the best. However, when the doctors made the decision to put Mom on a ventilator to assist her with breathing, I knew it was over, and Mom knew it too.

In true Mom fashion, she made a deal with the doctors and agreed to go on the ventilator if she could have a Diet Coke first, which was her favorite beverage and one she had been too sick to consume for the past two weeks. The doctors agreed, and the last moment we were alone together, I hugged her hard, and she whispered to me that she'd be watching me from above. Then she asked me to take care of Dad. Through the tears barreling down my face, I promised her I would.

The nurses rolled her down the hallway as she casually sipped Diet Coke through a plastic straw. That was the last conversation I had with Mom, who could no longer speak on the ventilator. She died

BE CONFIDENT IN YOUR CHOICES

two weeks later, after Dad and I made the horrifying decision to take her off the ventilator since she was declining and most of her organs were shutting down.

Uncle George visited while Mom was on the ventilator, and Lance made the trip to Myrtle Beach to say goodbye to Mom, even though she never actually regained consciousness before she passed. Corinne and Sara made the trip, too, along with Renee. They came to surround me with love as I said goodbye to my favorite person in the entire world.

Mom took her last breath just before noon on Saturday, February 28, 2015, surrounded by Dad, Lance, and me. She barely lasted two hours after the ventilator was removed, but those two hours were spent with her dearest loved ones. My therapist, Carol, had prepared me for this moment hours before as I sat in the hospital parking lot and poured my heart out to her over the phone. She told me that I had the strength to get through this, even though I didn't believe her at the time. But she was right, and her faith in me helped me pull myself together enough to get back inside and spend those final precious hours with my mom.

It all happened too quickly to fully hit me until after; the shock and horror were too much to process in the moment. All I could do was hold her hand as she exited the world, listening to her favorite music, the Rolling Stones, compliments of Corinne's iPad. You can't ask for too much more when you go, can you?

. . .

The days after Mom died were a blur of extreme despair and grief, mixed with lots of nutty Dad behavior. It started just hours after she died, with Dad demanding we gather for a sushi dinner at our family's favorite restaurant. Still stunned and numb, Lance, all my girls, and I were dragged to dinner to please Dad. Dad saw the dinner as a tribute to Mom, as something *she* would have wanted us to do.

I was too broken and exhausted to fight for my right to not party. I wanted to stay in and cry my eyes out because my mommy had just died. Instead, we went along, together with a large framed photo of Mom in her younger years. He placed the photo in her own chair; you should have seen the looks we got.

The next morning, I stumbled down Mom and Dad's hallway, which was now just Dad's hallway, disoriented as hell from this hard-hitting intro to grief. I'd been up most of the night, and in my delirium, I was confused by what I overheard.

Dad was on the phone, telling the person on the other end, "We're not flying Linda up to Maryland for her service; we're driving her."

I paused and replayed Dad's words in my head, trying to make sense of the statement. Surely, I'd misunderstood him due to my groggy state and lack of coffee. As it turns out, folks, I had not misunderstood him. He was dead set that he and I would drive Mom to Maryland, to be buried in the family cemetery just outside Washington, DC.

Everyone tried to talk him out of this ridiculous plan, but he was firm. Since Mom was afraid of flying, he adamantly refused our entreaties that her final trip on this earth be in a plane. As romantic as he tried to make it sound, I had strong suspicions that this was not at all about Mom's fear of flying. It seemed far more likely that Dad was trying to save the thousands of dollars it would cost to fly her body. Their finances were not in great shape, and he could spare his own pride by leaning into his dead wife's fear.

Regardless of his reasons, I was certain that someone would step in and stop his nonsense. It had to be illegal, I thought, to drive a dead body across state lines. I'm sure I'd seen that on *Dateline* once or in a movie. But alas, I found out that it was only illegal if you didn't have proper documentation for the dead body, or if, you know, you killed the person.

Anyway, Dad got his special certificate from the funeral home in Myrtle Beach, rented a cargo van from Enterprise, and insisted that I drive the van. Dad rode shotgun, and Mom was lying down in the back. Once again, I was too numb and quite frankly in too much shock to argue with Dad.

Dad couldn't drive because he would fall asleep behind the wheel if driving more than an hour at a time. Lance flat-out refused to ride in the van with Dad and Mom's dead body. So, it was up to me to pilot our final family road trip. Lance did kindly consent to accompany us in his own car.

I insisted he follow and put his little white Mercedes between us and any strangers who might rear-end us, not knowing Mom's casket was in the cargo hold. I had a terror that we'd be in an accident and Mom's body would be dislodged from the van and roll into traffic. Putting my brother as a buffer between my mother and other vehicles seemed like a good idea at the time.

It wasn't other drivers I needed to worry about, but the weather. The day Dad and I drove Mom's dead body to Maryland for her final pilgrimage and her funeral, which was scheduled for the next morning, the entire Eastern Seaboard experienced a freak snowstorm, in the beginning of March. It was big enough to be given its own name, Winter Storm Thor. Are you fucking kidding me?

Dad and I picked Mom up in the van from the funeral home in Myrtle Beach before dawn. The funeral home in Maryland gave me strict instructions to have her there by six that night; otherwise her funeral the next day would be canceled. No pressure, no pressure, just Winter Storm Thor, the storm of the century, an elderly man in front, my dead mom in the back, and a big-ass rental van ... This was going to be fine, right?

Lance followed us as promised, at first. However, I helplessly watched him angrily pass the van and drive off before we crossed South Carolina state lines. Why? Oh, because he and Dad got into it on the phone while we were driving.

I tried to remain calm as I white-knuckled the steering wheel, mom's wedding ring on my finger glinting in the headlights of oncoming traffic. I was terrified about the weather ahead as I advanced up the East Coast. I'm from the mild climate of the South, where I always drove compact cars. I had no idea how to drive a large cargo van through a snowstorm, much less with a body in the back. Dad passed the time by writing Mom's obituary, which I think I helped him with, but honestly, I can't be certain. It's a blur of stress and snow.

I've struggled with religion and my belief in God throughout my entire life. However, my faith took a boost from the fact that I made it to that funeral home in Maryland by ten to six. That I made it there at all—trudging through snow and ice, driving a van with my dead mother in the back, and enduring my living and highly argumentative father in the front—makes me think God might be a fan of mine.

When we arrived at the funeral home to drop off Mom, Lance opened the funeral home's side door and took me aside. He apologized for getting angry with Dad and leaving us like that. I had no words. I honestly still have no words. Relieved to have him back in the fold, we had new challenges. Mom's funeral service could no longer include a graveside portion at the end because of the cold and snowy weather. They wouldn't even be able to bury Mom for several weeks, until the ground thawed.

"Lovely," I thought. We were also told that we'd probably be unable to drive to the funeral home/cemetery in the morning because of the road conditions, which meant we'd have to take the train into DC/Maryland. I asked the folks at the funeral home if we should postpone the service a few days to allow the storm to pass through. They responded that we'd have to reschedule it to sometime in April because they were booked solid.

We decided to press on and have the service the next morning, mostly because of the people who had made the trip up here from afar, like Lance's family. Also, my McGee family was making their way through Winter Storm Thor as we were speaking. Above all, I just needed to get this over with.

Reunited, Lance drove the three of us to Uncle George and Aunt Hope's house an hour later to stay the night. The next morning, our group of a dozen, including two children and an elderly man who could barely walk, boarded the train to Union Station in Washington, DC, to bury Mom.

What we didn't know for sure but definitely suspected was that hardly anyone else would be at her funeral. Just getting to the train station was hazardous. The icy roads were treacherous. Once at the train station, Dad handed large black trash bags to Corinne, Lisa, Kim, Lance, and me.

What on earth were in the trash bags, you ask? Ceramic cats from my parents' home, which Dad claimed to be Mom's favorites. This decor was mandatory; he wanted ceramic cats all around the funeral home for her service. You know, the service that hardly anyone would attend.

We had to switch trains several times to get to Union Station. With each transfer, my sister-in-law, Laura, had to hold on to her father to ensure he didn't fall. I did the same with my dad, who was looking more frail by the minute. At Union Station, we had to hail three cabs to transport all of us, and the cats, to the funeral home, located just on the other side of the DC/Maryland line.

I'M SORRY I CREMATED YOU

Sandwiched in my cab with my girls and four bags of cats, I was blown away by the fact that these women were on this unimaginable journey with me. They were my best friends, yes, but an icy multi-transfer journey with hefty bags full of ceramic cat companions goes above and beyond best friend duties. The McGees had crossed over into full-fledged family, and I was so relieved that we were making our status official.

We were down one McGee, as Sara's flight into DC had been canceled due to Thor, and she was rerouted to NYC, where she spent the night all alone. Yet, she was determined to get to Mom's funeral, and she got up at an ungodly hour to catch a train from NYC to DC. Sara's whereabouts were unknown as we worried about her in the cab on the way to the funeral.

It was truly planes, trains, and automobiles to get all of us to that funeral home, and when we did, with five minutes to spare before the service was to start, we saw that there were only three additional friends of our family who made the trek. I couldn't help but think that Mom was watching us and laughing her ass off at the sheer ridiculousness of the situation. She was always such a prankster and probably had a hand in this.

We greeted those three beautiful and brave souls, signed the guest book, and placed the ceramic cats all over the funeral home. Before the service began, I spent a moment alone with Mom. Her casket was only open for a few minutes, and they would close it when the service began. In the vestibule, I looked at her, dressed in a classy outfit—going to her final rest in a silver top and chic black slacks. Classy McGee had helped me style Mom two days earlier.

Standing over her, I noticed that Dad had placed a photo collage of all Mom's cats throughout the years inside the casket beside her. I smiled and then reached down and squeezed Mom's hand, which felt cold and waxy. I didn't know what to say to her ... how to put a final punctuation mark on this relationship that meant absolutely everything to me. So, I spoke from my heart, saying, "I'll love you forever. Thanks for being the best mom in the whole world."

The service was beautiful; several of us spoke about Mom, including myself. I was too tired, numb, and shocked to cry. Grief autopilot left me feeling like I had to be strong in that moment because Dad was falling apart at the seams.

After the service, we gathered up the ceramic cats, hailed three more cabs, and backtracked to Union Station. In the train station, we ran into my sweet Sara. She had tried so hard to make it to Mom's funeral, to be by my side, and help hold me up. She was devastated to have missed it but finding her there at that minute meant everything to me. I wrapped my arms around her and cried the tears I had been needing to cry all morning. Sara was my safe space, and without my Mom I needed her exactly where she was at that moment.

• • •

I thrived at my technology company for eight years. Then came the global pandemic, and I was part of a massive 17 percent workforce reduction. Nothing like this had ever happened to me. The loss felt more like a death than a layoff. I didn't get out of bed for days and had no idea how I'd pay my mortgage. I kept telling myself that there had to be a deeper meaning behind all of it and that one day I'd look back and be happy that it happened, but I didn't believe it.

Fortunately, I landed a new gig within a couple of months, working for the federal government as an executive assistant. The feds were kind, and I had a steady paycheck. But I wasn't fulfilled. At all. The sterile environment was a shock after years with a tech company with seemingly endless resources. (I guess those resources weren't endless after all.) I was bored at work but thrilled to have a job. The pandemic was still raging, and I had no plans to job hop. Until ... I got a call from a recruiter at Advantage | Forbes Books nine months into my federal job.

They were a publishing company, their CEO needed an executive assistant, and they were interested in hiring me. I hemmed and hawed because I didn't want to leave the feds so soon, especially after they'd been so kind to me in my moment of need. But I decided to take an interview. I mean, what could it hurt, right? I had to at least give this company a chance since they reached out to *me*. Plus, I love books, so publishing sounded appealing!

The interview process was long, but the deeper I got into it, the more I wanted the job. Everyone was warm and sincere and deeply committed to their company culture, which aligned with my values. Also, I noticed the human resources department was rather small, so maybe I could get my foot in the door, do a great job, and get into human resources, where I knew I'd thrive.

Near the very end of the hiring process, someone casually mentioned a Team Member Book Publishing Program.

"A what?" I asked.

They explained that after an employee has been with the company at least one year, they become eligible to publish a manuscript with no cost to the employee. I took this information and tucked it into my figurative pocket. I accepted the job and went off to join the publishing world, in search of greener pastures and a warmer work environment.

After an exciting year working as the CEO's executive assistant, I accepted a new position in Team Member Success (our name for human resources), focusing on employee engagement, benefit management, and my favorite—company culture!

BE CONFIDENT IN YOUR CHOICES

Just a month after Dad died, I found myself back in my CEO's office, pitching this book idea and hoping he would allow me to be part of the Team Member Book Publishing Program. Spoiler alert: he said yes.

I was gutted by my layoff, but even though I didn't believe it at the time, it did lead to something better. Nothing is coincidental in life, folks. The stars aligned, the universe provided, and I ended up exactly where I was supposed to be. And I just bet Dad had his hand in it, somehow.

BE AFFECTED AND LET GO

Allowing yourself to be affected by the actions and words of your scene partners adds emotional depth to your character and the scene. Letting go of control is key in improv, as it allows the scene to unravel collaboratively and organically.

NOVEMBER 28, 2022

I am transitioning from level 3 to level 4 of improv, just as Dad is transitioning from this world to the next. Level 3 is taught by Ali, a woman who radiates warmth and kindness. She is like a Disney princess in the woods with animals surrounding her, only the animals are figments of an improv imagination. I want to be one of Ali's animals because of the calming warmth of her presence. Ali's class focuses on Relationship-Based Scene Work. Each level at Theatre 99 is designed to get more intense, and this class does not disappoint. We have to truly connect with our scene partners and express emotions and vulnerability, and the stretch is jarring for some of my classmates. It isn't jarring for me. I love it. I need it. I crave connection, even if it is in improv.

We explore the history between the characters on stage, and Ali encourages us to direct thoughts toward our scene partners, like "I am the way I am because of you, and you are the way you are because of me ... because of our history together." I can't help but think of how this relates to my complicated relationship with Dad and the rich history we've shared since the day I was born, and the fact that I am the way I am largely because of him.

Ali teaches us the importance of being affected by our scene partners. One night she has each of us take the stage with a partner and pantomime a game of silent tennis. We have to demonstrate emotions when returning the ball to our partner, and then our partner has to react to that emotion.

Improv is the pure magic of the human imagination working in concert. There we are, make-believe balls flying through the air and grown-ass humans swatting at them with all their might, wiping phantom sweat off our faces ... or is it real? We do this over and over until each of us is exhausted from our pretend tennis match and the emotions we lob back and forth.

It is impossible not to notice the parallels between the vulnerability I embrace in improv and the vulnerability I endure outside improv, grieving the loss of the most important man in my life. Improv, which again, started as a bucket list item I wanted to check off, is now a form of therapy I desperately need to get through losing Dad.

At the end of each level at Theatre 99, we have a recital night for our family and friends, and a few other random audience members, and level 3 is no different. What is different is that the recital is one week after Dad's death, and I am still in shock from the entire experience. Nobody expects me to show up the night of our recital, but I do. Because I have to. For myself.

BE AFFECTED AND LET GO

Not only do I feel the need to officially finish the class I started seven weeks ago, and poured so much of myself into, but I also need the distraction. I need to take the stage with my classmates, who have become my friends, and take the form of a character that is not myself. I need to express my feelings and emotions by taking the form of someone else. I need to be affected and have someone else affected by me. I need to get up there on that stage and for a few short minutes be completely unable to think about the fact that the man I love more than anything is gone.

The show is great, or so I am told. I don't remember much. Everything from that time is a blur, but I do remember Ali sending me a text after the show, telling me that she is so sorry to hear about Dad, that she is here if I ever need to talk, and that she is tremendously impressed that I showed up for our class recital.

I respond by telling her how much her class and her words mean to me and that the recital is exactly what this grieving daughter needed. She needs to connect with something, anything, other than death.

DECEMBER 17, 2022

Wearing a borrowed dress, I'm relieved to have Dylan, looking dapper in his black suit and tie and resembling a secret service agent, at my side to say goodbye to my dad. He's my anchor preventing me from falling adrift in the seemingly endless sea of navy-blue chairs in a Myrtle Beach megachurch as we attend Dad's celebration of life.

With him by my side, I have a buffer for loneliness and despair that would otherwise drown me. Dylan is a bulwark protecting me from the judgments, or my fear of the judgments I assume others would hold against me without a man by my side for Dad's funeral. This formal setting seems like the type of life event that requires a plus-one. At Mom's funeral seven years before, I felt like the pathetic and forever single spinster. Even with my girls, who were more than enough, churches and funerals seemed to demand a traditional pairing.

Sara is directly behind me, flanked by several of my incredible friends who have become my chosen family. Among these I count Brian and Kimber, who came into my life through workplaces we've left behind, artifacts on our collective résumés. Yet, our friendships have endured and deepened over the years. These "salt of the earth" people literally have my back, and I look over my shoulder at them with love and gratitude. I also see Kimberly, Alia, and Tammi taking their seats in solidarity. So many beautiful people drove all the way from Charleston to support me, and this truth brings more tears to my misty eyes.

The church bells chime at 11:00 a.m., and the doors to the auditorium close. Tom, one of Dad's closest friends, takes the podium. Tom is the church's musical director, and Dad loved coming here the last few years. Tom offered his church and handled most of the details for this celebration of life; no one is calling it a funeral.

After the past year, I am immensely relieved that one of the few things I have to coordinate is arranging the military honors for Dad today. That is an easy task. After sending them a copy of Dad's military discharge papers, all I have to do is ensure that Lance and I are sitting next to each other so the soldiers can present the flag to us, Dad's surviving children. I also have to bring Dad, in the form of ashes, of course.

Tom welcomes the attendees. When I look around the auditorium, I try not to feel disappointed that more people didn't show up to honor Dad. He was so beloved in the community, and I was expecting more of a crowd for him, at least as big as at his estate sale.

Dad would have loved a big crowd, but he would have loved to not be cremated too.

Tom says a few words and then introduces the two military officers who wait just outside. The doors open, and two soldiers in full military uniform soberly march in step down the main aisle. When the soldiers reach the end of the aisle, they stop abruptly. Taps begins to play, and I'm hit hard by the gravity of this situation and the profound emotional impact of the melody. I can hardly breathe.

I clutch the armrests of my seat as tightly as I can without physically breaking them, and swallow, trying to hold myself together. "I can do this," I think to myself. "I drove my dead mother's body to her funeral through a freaking snowstorm, so surely I can hold myself together long enough to get through this song. I will not break down. I will be strong."

Certain I'm about to lose it and break down into a sobbing mess, I notice something about the soldiers. One soldier is standing tall holding a full military salute while the other plays taps on his trumpet. Only ... he's not. He's playing at playing the trumpet, like Milli Vanilli or Ashley Simpson lip-syncing on *Saturday Night Live*. He's not air guitaring, he's air trumpeting to a recording of taps emanating from some mysterious source.

I catch on because he's holding the trumpet to his lips but not blowing into it. His fingers barely move as he touches the instrument. This strikes me as both disappointing and humorous. Later, I learn there are too many baby-boomer veteran funerals and not enough Gen Z soldier trumpeters. It's a human resource problem. Too many soccer moms, not enough trumpet moms out there.

After taps I exhale for what feels like the first time in several minutes. The soldiers are in motion, choreographed to perfection, and then they are standing directly in front of Lance and me, folding an

American flag with solemn precision, resulting in the perfect triangle. One of the soldiers extends his arms and tries to hand the perfectly folded triangle to either Lance or me, but neither of us moves to accept it. Lance looks at me, and I look at him. I'm still frozen, overwhelmed by the taps experience, so Lance accepts the triangle and thanks the soldiers, who then march out of the auditorium, probably off to another funeral.

Tom leads the Lord's Prayer, then tells endearing stories about Dad. In a recent story, Dad wrote a very special letter to God. His first draft wasn't enough, so Dad pursued a crusade to perfect his prayer, eventually hanging it in his room at the VVH. He'd roped Lance into transcribing the letter and roped me into printing it, resulting in so many versions that I finally had to get firm with Dad and tell him he was killing too many trees, and this was the final, final version, period.

After I refused more revisions, Dad demanded that the letter be printed on a particular kind of paper, in a particular font, which reminded me of his Things Remembered purchase. Even Tom got drafted to create artwork for the letter.

Finally, I got the letter printed at Kinkos, went over to Michaels craft store and blew a ridiculous amount of money on a twenty-four by thirty-six-inch gold frame I hoped Dad would find acceptable to encapsulate his letter to God. Just so you know, he was never fully satisfied with the framed letter because he said it wasn't the latest and greatest version.

Listening to Tom tell the story, I glance at the enormous framed letter to God, on full display next to Tom. I wonder if I could have been a better daughter. Maybe I could have been more patient about the letter and about everything ... maybe I could have found a way to bring Dad into my home, instead of putting him in the nursing

BE AFFECTED AND LET GO

home. My eyes sting, but I fight with all my might to hold my tears back. I will not let myself fall apart.

Scriptures are read, more prayers are said, and music plays too loudly through the speakers of the cavernous auditorium. Tom begins to passionately sing into his handheld microphone. I didn't realize Tom was going to sing today, but it makes sense, since he's the musical director of the church. Tom loved Dad, so of course he will honor him in this way.

I remain stoic, as I've planned, until I listen closer to the words Tom is singing. Snippets of the lyrics break into my thoughts, lyrics like, "I'm walking in streets of gold … I'm splashing in the crystal sea … rubies and diamonds don't mean a thing."

I glance to my right at Dylan, who is also stoic, and he offers me a gentle half smile. But this song incites a strange reaction in me, and I'm not sure why. The lyrics seem over the top to me. Maybe they're not; maybe it's just me because I'm not a deeply religious person. Spiritual, yes. Religious, no.

"Sapphires and pearls scatter around, but they don't compare to the beautiful sound of angels singing praise to my Lord." And with that lyric, despite all my energy spent trying to prevent myself from crying hysterically, I am not prepared for a different kind of outburst. Instead of sobbing, I erupt into the biggest laughing fit of my entire life, right there in the middle of my dad's celebration of life during Tom's song.

Dylan looks at me, startled by the inappropriate laughter pouring out of my body at this solemn moment. Our eyes lock, and suddenly Dylan is laughing with me, though he's not sure what we're laughing about. I'm cackling now, trying to keep it as quiet as possible because, even as I've lost control, I *know* this is not acceptable behavior, but I'm unable to stop.

Tears run down my cheeks as the laughing continues, and I'm desperately trying to pretend like I'm sobbing from the anguish of Dad's passing and not laughing hysterically. What the hell is happening to me? Dylan puts his left arm around my shoulder, half trying to console me and half trying to pretend like both of us are deeply grieving. But I can't stop laughing.

I'm praying nobody can hear my wails of laughter or see it on my face, but I look back at Kimber and Sara, and their eyes widen as they realize what's happening to me. They both instantly look away from me in an effort to keep themselves from catching the contagion of my laughter.

I laugh and cry through the rest of Tom's beautiful song, and I feel terrible about it, but there's just no stopping it. It's as though all the tears I've been holding back today and all the days leading up to this moment are escaping in the form of laughter, and I can't stop it.

The silver lining is that even though people in the audience have noticed, I don't think Tom does, as he is engrossed in his song and in the moment, thank the Lord. When Tom has finished singing and I'm absolutely drained from my indiscreet emotional breakdown, it's time for me to stand up and eulogize Dad.

I retrieve my journal from beneath my seat and take the stage. Somehow, I'm composed, stoic, somber, and calm, and I talk about how Dad did everything in life big, just like his letter to God. This letter that he actually asked me once to have mass-produced and sold to the public, all profits going to Tom's church. I talk about the fact that Dad was so passionate about the fight against Alzheimer's that he turned his house into a donation site and strung signs up in the front yard.

I hear a lot of laughter from the crowd as I talk about his Christmas lists over the last few years, which included the following items: Gold Toe socks, Stetson aftershave, caviar, muffuletta, peanuts with salt, brown corduroy pants, and shotgun shells.

I keep looking down at my leather-bound journal to remember what I want to say. I talk about how passionate Dad was about golf and how he gave many nurses and doctors free golf lessons, whether they wanted them or not, while he was in the Grand Strand Hospital for three months earlier this year.

I talk about what the heartbreak this year has been like, for both Dad and me. Yet, I also testify to how lucky I was to be with Dad as he passed away a few weeks ago. And then I read the following notes from my journal:

"Nobody will ever love me like my dad loved me, and there is an enormous hole in my heart that will be there forever. I like to think that he's in heaven now, reunited with my mom, and that they are dancing like they used to do, and probably also eating big bowls of butter pecan ice cream. Rest easy, Dad. I'll live big for you and will always try to help others, in your honor."

Moments before the service ends, the song that Dad asked me, when I was a child, to play at his funeral one day begins playing through the auditorium speakers. It's not a Sinatra song—it's "Centerfield" by John Fogerty—and it brings fresh tears to my eyes, just as the last round has dried.

A slideshow Tom helped me create is projected on a big screen. The auditorium is now full of photos from Dad's seventy-nine years on this earth. Through my tears, I smile and look up toward the ceiling of the auditorium, knowing I've made Dad happy with this song and the entire celebration of life. It's exactly what he would have wanted, minus the laughing fit and the fact that his body is now ashes.

I'M SORRY I CREMATED YOU

DECEMBER 19, 2022

The floor of my darling little Park Circle house is covered in cardboard boxes that my friend Matt purchased from Home Depot. He drove all the way here to Charleston from Atlanta. Matt and I have been friends since middle school, and he called me two days ago to see if I needed help with my move, because that's just the kind of big-hearted and selfless friend he is.

Move, you ask? Why on earth would I be moving away from the neighborhood I adore, just weeks after losing my father? Well, you see, I've managed to build up a decent amount of debt this year (OK, fine, I had some from the previous year as well), starting with three months of living off and on in a Hampton Inn, as well as other travel and expenses related to Dad.

One night a month ago, I was lying in bed, not able to sleep because of the financial stress bearing down upon me, when I suddenly sat up in bed, realizing that there was an easy solution to my problems: my house. Park Circle had really become a hot spot to live in over the past few years, and I suspected I'd bought my home at the right time.

Also, I have no business owning an old home built in the 1940s because I'm not handy whatsoever and don't have the extra money to renovate it like I had hoped. The stress of everything breaking around me on a daily basis was only adding to my financial stress, and all of it had become too much for me to handle. When I called my mortgage lender the next morning, he confirmed that it was indeed a fantastic time to sell and that I would make a pretty penny off the deal, which I planned to use to pay off my debt, throwing the rest into savings.

So here Matt and I sit, surrounded by boxes, packing up my life and memories and putting color-coded sticky notes on each box, mapping it to a new room in my new town house. That's how damn organized Matt is, and I love the hell out of him for it. (Spoiler alert:

I will soon find out that one of the two movers I have hired is color blind.)

Sara's come over for the packing party, and the three of us are packing up the kitchen. I leave them to it, and I venture into the guest bedroom, which contains all the family memories I rescued from Dad's house. Not just my family memories, but also Mom's and Dad's cherished memories from their families and their childhoods. I look around at the items and feel an enormous amount of pressure being the sole person responsible for them.

I sit on the floor and look through a box that has been in the guest room closet for years. This one contains all the souvenirs from Mom's death—the funeral program, the itty-bitty cards from the funeral flower arrangements that were sent, and the cards sent to me from family and friends.

Then I see the "dash memorial" that Dad wrote in honor of Mom shortly after she died. A dash memorial, for those unaware like I was, honors the life and legacy of a person, focusing on the life and achievements that occurred during the "dash" of their life. The dash refers to the dash that appears between a person's birth date and death date on their headstone. It's a way of celebrating the dash that symbolizes the totality of a life. I thought it was weird and senseless when Dad wrote it, but looking at it now, I'm ecstatic to have a physical item detailing Mom's life from beginning to end.

As I describe this dash memorial, it's important for you, dear reader, to understand that Dad was always a little odd and eccentric, but once Mom died his eccentricities were elevated to another level ... a level I didn't even know was possible. The front and back cover of the dash memorial is a replica of Mom and Dad's favorite flowery wallpaper from their home in Myrtle Beach, printed professionally and in color, as is the rest of the booklet, which contains twenty illustrated pages of Mom's life.

For the rest of my life, I will never forget when Dad came to me with the first version of the dash memorial and asked me to edit it. It was a couple of months after Mom died, and I was in no mood to read about her life. I was still trying to survive her death. Nonetheless, I accepted the booklet from Dad, and I began to read.

The dash starts off nicely, detailing Mom's childhood, including her favorite childhood pets: two French poodles named Bandy and Jeri and a rabbit named Thumper whom I'd never heard of before. Dad even talks about the church where Mom was baptized and the actual playground she played on as a child. This man did his research!

Dad then goes into Mom's first marriage to her high school sweetheart, Lance's birth, and the heartbreaking death of Lance's father when he was a small child. Next Dad writes how he "received his greatest lifetime gift, meeting Linda at a Christmas party held at his Southern Towers apartment in Washington, DC" and says, "After six months of steady dating, Linda and Shelby began a lifetime journey of love and dedication to each other."

Everything's going well in the memorial until page three, where Dad begins to physically describe Mom: "Linda's physical beauty was awesome from head to toe. Her 5'8", 122-pound curvaceous body (37-23-35) was the essence of femininity and sexuality for her lucky husband. Just holding hands, a tender caress, or a close hug conveyed real joy and that feeling of love. More intimate time and tender kisses, and the ecstasy of lovemaking was very special."

"*Whoa, what the hell, Dad?*" I said loudly, indicating my shock at what I'd just read. I pointed to the part of the paragraph that had just shaken me to my core, and Dad looked at me, confused as to why I was having this reaction to the material.

"First of all, you cannot list out Mom's body measurements in this thing, and you absolutely cannot, under any circumstances, talk about your sex life, ugh! And furthermore, who exactly is going to get copies of this?" I asked, completely disgusted and annoyed.

"Everyone who knew your mother," Dad said calmly. "All of our family and all of our friends over the years."

I handed the booklet back to Dad and said that I would not continue reading this or help with editing until everything inappropriate was removed. Dad compromised by removing the line about their "lovemaking" (I just threw up in my mouth saying that word in reference to my parents), but despite my protests, he left in Mom's measurements.

Now, eight years later, sitting on the floor of my guest bedroom with both of my parents gone, I'm grateful to have the dash memorial and will cherish it forever. Isn't it funny how grief changes a person? I think about how many quiet, reflective moments I have now, with flashes of my old life constantly appearing before my eyes. The intensity of those flashes takes my breath away for just a moment.

Most people probably don't notice when these quiet moments overtake me, but those chosen family members of mine who truly know me see it.

I stand up and grab another box from the closet to sort through before I sit down on the bed.

The bed. Dad was the last person to sleep in this bed, a little over a year ago, which happens to be the very event that kicked off this god-awful dying year. Dad stayed with me for a week just before Thanksgiving 2021 because he had fallen on his porch while unplugging Christmas lights at three in the morning. In the fall, he broke his kneecap. His buddy, Tom, took him to the emergency room the next morning. Then Tom drove Dad halfway to Charleston to stay with me and recuperate while he couldn't put any pressure on his knee or live alone. I was petrified to have him become my responsibility, for several reasons, including the five stairs Dad had to mount to enter my house and the fact that his behavior and forgetfulness during this time were becoming seriously worrisome.

On my way to meet Tom and Dad at the halfway point, I stopped at a medical supply store and purchased things I thought would be good to have. My purchases included a portable handicapped toilet, in case Dad couldn't make it to the bathroom and needed the toilet in the guest bedroom. The toilet came with rails that would help Dad stand up and sit down and contained a plastic bucket under the seat, which I assumed I would have to dump after each use. God help me.

I pulled off the side of the road just outside Mcclellanville, South Carolina, to meet Tom and Dad. Tom, a big, strong man, had no trouble getting Dad from his truck into the passenger seat of my car. However, I had no clue how I was going to get him out of my car at my house and up those front steps.

Dad and I drove the forty-five minutes back to my house in silence, mostly because Dad was in so much pain. I was thankful we made it home before dark outside, as the drive between Mcclellanville and Charleston is quite rural, and I always worried about hitting a deer.

I breathed a little sigh of relief as I pulled into my driveway, but not a big sigh because I still had to get Dad up those damn front stairs. I stepped out of the car and walked around to the passenger side to assist Dad. When I tell you that it took an hour to get Dad out of that car, I am not exaggerating. He was in so much pain, and my Honda Civic sat low to the ground, making it almost impossible for Dad to get out of the car.

When Dad finally made it out of the car, we then had to get him up the walkway and up the stairs. Just getting him up the walkway was a feat. He had his arm around my shoulders the whole time, leaning on me for support to avoid putting weight on his knee.

We were a mere three feet away from the front stairs when Dad suddenly proclaimed, "I have to take a shit, Jaclyn."

"OK, Dad, we just have to get you up the stairs and into the house so that you can use the restroom," I said confidently, as if I didn't believe it would be a difficult task at all.

"No, I mean right now, right here," Dad said, and I suddenly heard the urgency in his voice.

Panic hit me like a ton of bricks, and I had no idea what to do. I looked at Dad but could see that at this moment, the only thing he knew was that he was about to defecate on my front walkway. I couldn't just pick Dad up and quickly get him inside because I wasn't capable of lifting him. "Fuck! What should I do?" I thought.

At that moment I remembered the portable handicapped toilet I had in the back seat of my car, and I ran as fast as I could to grab it. I knew by the look on Dad's face that I didn't have time to set it up, but I could at least grab the plastic bucket for him to go in, which I did.

I raced back to Dad with the bucket in my hand, saying, "Here, use this!" Then I noticed that Dad had already unbuttoned and dropped his tan corduroy pants, which were pooled around his ankles. He was already working on getting his boxer shorts down.

I was in hell. This was actually hell.

I positioned the bucket under Dad's rear end and left it there on the ground as I ran to the outskirts of my front yard, maybe hoping to stop any traffic that was coming down the road? I didn't even know what I was doing at that point besides straight-up panicking and freaking the hell out.

What if a neighbor saw Dad shitting in a bucket in front of my house? What if I saw Dad shitting in a bucket in front of my house? I couldn't see that!

Then tears filled my eyes, and I began to cry, utterly unable to handle this situation anymore. I needed help.

I took my cell phone out of the pocket of my jeans, and I scrolled to my neighbor Lauren, who lived two doors down with her boyfriend, Rob. They'd become good friends of mine since we kinda sorta went through a pandemic together. I certainly didn't believe our friendship was close enough for her to see my dad shitting in the front yard, but desperate times …

I dialed Lauren's number, and she answered on the second ring, cheerfully. I cried into the phone, telling her my dad was here, he had a broken kneecap, and I needed help right now. I didn't have to say another word, as Lauren knew all about Dad and the difficulties that came along with him. She told me she was with Rob and our incredible neighbors, Rachel and John, and that they'd be here in five minutes to help.

I hung up the phone and glanced back at Dad as quickly as I could, in an effort to see only as much as necessary and still as little as possible. He was still hovering in the shitting position, pants and boxers around his ankles.

I was crying in frustration and helplessness, crying that things had gotten so bad with Dad that I had to see him taking a shit in front of my house. I was humiliated for him and myself and was more than relieved when a white truck pulled up to my house with my extraordinary neighbors, who had become close friends, ready to help me through this literally shitty situation.

I must have blocked the details of what happened next. I remember crying frantically and explaining the situation to my friends, who took control of the situation and simply handled it. I remember pulling up Dad's boxers and pants and discovering that he wasn't able to get all the feces inside the bucket. It was all over my walkway. I remember Rob and Lauren taking charge of Dad and carrying him up the stairs and into the house, and I remember Rachel and John taking my hose and cleaning the bucket and my walkway, so that I didn't have to.

I remember telling Rachel not to do that because I felt so embarrassed, and she said to me, "Nobody should have to clean up their own father's poop. We got this; go inside."

The week that followed this incident was brutal. I wasn't capable of lifting Dad, which made things even more difficult, and Lauren and Rob often came over to assist. I learned Lauren had experience in working with the elderly and was trained in lifting and transporting them, which was a true godsend. Rachel and John were always nearby, too, when I needed them, as well as Justin and Caitlin, other neighbors of mine that became close friends during the pandemic and the couple of years that followed.

After a week of caring for Dad's every need but not truly being able to give him the care he needed (he hadn't even had a bath since he arrived), I sat on the edge of the very bed I'm sitting on right now and told him things had to change. I told him I was taking him to the hospital the next day so that he could get the care he needed and deserved.

Then I told him that when he got out of the hospital, it was officially time for him to go into the independent living facility I had found for him here in Charleston so that I could be closer to him and help him. I told him I knew it wasn't what he wanted, but if he didn't listen to me and allow me to help care for him, he was going to soon end up in a nursing home or in the grave, which is exactly what happened, in that order.

I called an ambulance the next morning to come take Dad out of the house and get him to the hospital. He recovered nicely there for a week or so, but then he insisted upon going home, by himself, and not into the independent living facility I set up for him. On the day he was discharged from the hospital, I looked at him and said that if he did this, I would no longer be here to help because it was too difficult, it wasn't fair to me or him, and the stress and anxiety was taking an unfair toll on me.

He looked at me like I was a petulant child and sternly declared that he was going home. I walked out of the hospital, and an ambulance transported him back to Myrtle Beach. He was carried back into his house on a stretcher and left to take care of himself. A month later, in January 2022, I would receive the call from the hospital in Myrtle Beach telling me Dad had been found incoherent in his recliner, soaked in his own urine.

His decision to refuse appropriate assistance or to take appropriate planning cost us both so much, including my home in the supportive neighborhood that helped me care for him in the first place.

MAY 18, 2023

I sit on the couch in the green room of Theatre 99, waiting to hit the stage with my level 5 class for our final class recital. There are only five levels of curriculum at Theatre 99, and I've now completed all five of them, along with the other beautiful humans in this room. Most of my cohort went through all five levels together with me.

This is my last recital, and I can't believe I made it, especially with everything that has occurred since I started classes here. I suspect, though, that my time here, escaping into humor, creativity, and camaraderie, helped me make it through the difficult things outside the theater.

Many of my friends are in the audience, along with Dylan, waiting for me to go on stage and perform improv. I can't help but think of everything these friends have helped me through the past year and a half.

Sadly, I also can't help but think about how difficult my relationship with Dylan has become, since he is hardly ever in Charleston. When he is here, now that we know each other better, it seems we don't have too much in common. Discovering each other is always an exciting adventure, but that adventure can terminate quickly when your shared interests reach an impasse. Still, I'm happy he's here tonight, and it means a lot to me that he made me a priority.

I grin from ear to ear when I reflect on how much fun I've had here at Theatre 99, during some of the roughest times of my life. This place, and improv in itself, have become a form of therapy for me, a way to escape everything else going on in my life. I'm forced to be present in the moment when I'm onstage and not think about any of the stress or grief I've been dealing with. Honestly, I only intended to take the level 1 class, to check it off my bucket list, and move on to the next thing. Now I cannot imagine my life without improv in it.

When my level 5 class started a few months ago, we had to do a warm-up exercise with a partner we didn't know well. I got this guy named Fred as a partner, and the exercise was for Fred to ask me what my biggest fear is in life, and then I was to ask him the same question.

I hadn't really thought about this question in years, and I realized at that moment that losing my parents was always my biggest fear in life, but that had already happened to me. I couldn't think of another big fear. Somehow, after surviving my greatest, I came out on the other side a better person, a wiser person, a deeper person. I was someone who has been privy to the darkest moments life has to offer and survived it. Standing with Fred, I was overwhelmed by how tragically beautiful that is.

As we prepare for this final recital in the green room, I consider all the life lessons improv has taught me. It's so much more than being funny. Improv has taught me how to handle my anxiety better because it taught me to embrace rather than fear the unknown. Improv is all about the unknown and what's going to happen next. Improv is a magical alchemy that transforms paralyzing anxiety into exhilarating anticipation.

I've had to learn to embrace that and even enjoy it. This transformation in me is priceless and has taught me that living in the moment is a pleasure worth pursuing. I'm so much better at it now.

Improv has also nurtured my self-confidence. Without it, I would never have had the confidence to initiate a conversation with Dylan the night we met. Well, improv and the feeling that Mom somehow entered my body and made me do it through the influence of her Stones record.

Improv has also raised my communication game, personally and professionally. When doing a scene on stage with a scene partner, it's imperative that I listen intently to what my partner says. This skill was sharpened through exercises where we could only respond to the last thing our partner said using the last letter of the last word they said to initiate our response to them. A live-action sestina, dual and dueling poetry in motion. To make that magic, we had to hang on every word our partner said. It was an art, and it could be practiced in every interaction.

I thought improv was fun and funny, but I never knew it was an artform that would teach me so many incredible life lessons or make me a stronger person. I don't know what the future holds for me with improv, but I do know that it's changed me for the better, and I'm grateful for everyone I've met along this journey.

On this night, we all stand up and create a circle in the green room to prepare ourselves before we take the stage. The circle is a ritual, like a prayer or a meditation, and each time we gather, we look around the circle, into each other's eyes, and one by one we go around to every person and put our hand on each other's shoulder, saying, "I've got your back out there."

At this moment, the last time we will do this as a class, I realize again that life is like improv, and I'm forever grateful for those in my life who have had my back and continue to do so. I never found the North Star from Dad's yard, which was a real bummer, but through improv, growth, and grief—and coming out of it on the other side an even better version of myself—I discovered that I'm my own North Star. I will always look for the funny in all life's moments, even the inappropriate ones, which is how I'll survive them. Well, that and with the support of my girls.

OCTOBER 3, 2023

Nearly a year after he died, I begin planning Dad's final burial and reunion with Mom, for the day after Thanksgiving. Nothing says Happy Turkey Day like opening up your mom's grave and stacking your dad's urn on top!

This reunion requires many phone calls to the funeral home and cemetery in Maryland. However, it's the first phone conversation with Paul, my funeral home liaison, that really tickles me. I've already explained to Paul that Mom, as well as many other family members, are buried up there in "his" cemetery and that when Mom died about eight years ago, Dad put his name next to hers on her headstone (along with some interesting illustrations of cats because … why wouldn't he?), with the plan of being buried there, with her, in the same grave.

Paul is not quite grasping everything I'm telling him over the phone, and he tries to make sense of the situation. Finally, he gets it. "Ohhhh, so your mom is already here with us," he says, as if he's the maître d' at a Michelin-star restaurant who's already seated my mother at her reserved table and is ready to complete the party.

"Yes," I say, "she sure is." Then I give Paul Mom's name for the third time.

Paul finally locates Mom in the computer system, and I hear the excitement in his voice when he says, "Wonderful! It looks like your mom is in a double-depth grave, which is perfect, so we can fit your dad in there too!"

I, trying to match Paul's enthusiasm and hide my shock at the term *double-depth grave*, parrot his enthusiasm and say, "Fantastic!"

Paul then asks, "How will the deceased be prepared for burial?"

"Huh?" I ask. Now I am the one not understanding the question.

"In what form will your father come to us?" Paul says.

"Ohhhh," I say, "he was cremated, so I'll be bringing his ashes, in an urn." And I cringe at the thought that this is not the form Dad wanted to take as he lies on top of Mom for eternity.

Paul then explains that I'll need to purchase an urn vault to hold the urn underground. He tells me he'll set up the minister from the funeral home to do the "graveside committal service," and I like Paul's classy choice of wording. Paul then tells me that the urn vault, the minister, a tent, and twelve chairs for the family, along with the opening and closing of the "site" will only cost us $2,494.

I almost spit out my coffee when I hear the total. I want to throw Paul's classy words back with a "Hell no, Paul, that's ridiculous!" However, after all the antics of an American medicalized death, I do realize my only other option is to bring a garden trowel to Maryland and dig a hole in the dark of night, like those people who leave roses on Poe's grave, but less romantic. I'm just not stoked about a drive-by ash drop, so I swallow my coffee and fake a chipper response to Paul, "Great!"

My next challenge is figuring out how I'm to transport Dad's ashes up to Maryland. Of course, I contemplate driving him there, carrying on the tradition of driving my parents through many states, to their final resting places. But I'd rather fly to Maryland, to save time and the pain of a late-autumn drive through unpredictable weather.

My choices are to bring Dad on the plane with me or ship him to Maryland. Taking him on the plane feels like the thing to do, since traveling with Dad's ashes would make a hell of a story. But I'm tired. And I don't really feel like manufacturing a story when the organic ones are more than sufficient. I just want to get this done and bury Dad as quickly and as easily as possible. No muss, no fuss, so I decide to ship his ashes.

I also don't want to engage in super awkward conversation with a US Postal Service worker about what exactly I'm trying to ship. It's not explosive, electric, perishable, or a lithium battery; it's just my dead Dad … I don't want to insure his ashes, have him lost in the dead letters department, or be told I'm not allowed to use the postal service to transport human cremains.

Instead, I call Simplicity, the helpful and caring folks who took Dad's body out of the VVH, transported him to their crematory, and handed him back to me in the form of ashes. His ashes were stored in a deep-blue titanium urn, with the US Navy seal on it, which Lance selected and sent to Simplicity, so I didn't have to collect my dad in a plastic bag. I like to think if Dad had wanted to be cremated, which we know he didn't, he would have liked that urn.

The kind lady at Simplicity tells me she'll take care of the whole thing for me, even though it has been almost a year since Dad was cremated, and I don't need to worry about anything. She asks me to bring Dad, along with a copy of his death certificate, to the crematory, and for the low, low price of $160, she will send Dad up to Maryland via Priority Mail. I assume he will have tracking and insurance in that package.

The next week I carry Dad's ashes in his urn to Simplicity, almost like I'd carry a baby on my hip. Though Dad doesn't get a car seat for the ride, I most certainly do buckle him up in the front passenger seat next to me. I walk into the crematory (what a weird word), with Dad bouncing on my hip, and I say to the woman who politely greets me, "He's been giving me a lot of trouble lately, and I'm here to give him back."

The woman looks at me with complete shock, and I chuckle and say, "I'm kidding. I'm Jaclyn Smith, and you guys are supposed to send my dad's ashes up to Maryland for me."

NOVEMBER 24, 2023

I sit in the uncomfortable metal folding chair under the rented tent for another somber occasion. It's the morning after Thanksgiving, and our Black Friday is spent in a cemetery, not a shopping mall, but this costs a lot more than any shopping excursion I've ever experienced. I'm looking into Mom's opened grave while Dad's urn is placed on top of her casket like a vase on a coffee table. It was technically more complicated, but that's the gist of it.

Dylan is not by my side. I ended our relationship a few months back. Dylan is a great man, and I learned so much from him and

BE AFFECTED AND LET GO

treasure happy memories and experiences from our one-year relationship. The truth is, he doesn't want to be a partner.

I fell in love with him, but he wasn't able to meet my emotional needs. Dylan was full of fun times, epic trips, good food, and wine but couldn't offer me what I truly wanted—a deep love that could sustain itself outside of travel and food.

Breaking up with Dylan was one of the hardest things I've ever done because I didn't want to do it. I wanted him to step up and be the man I needed him to be. I needed him to be more romantic, to care more, and to be crazy in love with me, but he wasn't that man.

Maybe he used to be in the past for another woman, but his own life held its own history of heartbreaks, and our timing was off. I stalled on ending our relationship because I felt like Mom had sent him to me, which had to mean he was my forever person. Then I finally figured out that she did send him to me, not to be my forever person but to be an incredible distraction for me during one of the worst years of my life. She knew I needed him to help me through losing Dad, and he did that.

Dylan served an important and deeply meaningful role in the improv that was the comic tragedy of 2022, and for that I'm forever grateful and will never regret our relationship. He also proved to me that I wasn't dead inside after all, like I had feared, and I was strong enough to seek what I needed and let him go when I realized he wasn't it.

I took so much from my relationship with Dylan, like the fact that I finally quit vaping. I quit for him, but I also quit for me, and I couldn't be happier about it. I write this while I suck on the Nicorette lozenge in my mouth (don't judge me, folks). Dylan took me to places I've only dreamed of, and he taught me how to shit in a bucket while camping, so I will never have to worry about shitting on a sidewalk because of my aim.

Dylan also served me my first ever glass of Dom Perignon—how about that for a juxtaposition? I learned to love again. Even if it was not a forever love, it was real, and it was worthwhile for as long as it lasted.

Instead of Dylan, Uncle George sits next to me. I'm eternally grateful for him, and Mom must be so happy that I've remained close to her little brother. Lance sits on my other side, and I'm grateful for him too—for him helping me when I needed him and being here at the end of this journey with Dad. Our relationship remains complicated, but I'm hopeful about what the future holds for us.

I look down at my hands and twist Dad's wedding ring on my left thumb and see Mom's wedding ring on my right ring finger. Adding Dad's ring has given me great peace, like they are reunited in my flesh, flesh they created together.

I think about both of them being with me, through their rings, when I'm doing mundane things like cooking dinner or planting flowers. Their rings remind me how much they loved each other and how much they loved me. This love goes on, even if they are no longer physically present.

I stand to say a few words as Dad's urn is lowered into the grave. I say that Dad was one of a kind with the biggest heart of anyone I've ever known, and then I say once again, "I'll live big for you, Dad. Now go be with Mom."

As our small family walks to our cars, my sister-in-law, Laura, hugs me. She tells me that I was such a great daughter and hands me a brown paper bag. I look at it, questioningly, and she says, "I found something in your dad's house I know you would want. You must have missed it when you went through the house."

I carefully open the bag and pull out "The Power of You" poem I plagiarized back in 1991, triggering Dad's endless obsession with my writing. I laugh uncontrollably; nobody in my family, including

Laura, knows I didn't write it. Nobody knows that I left this damn poem in Dad's house for a reason. I never wanted to see it again. But it found me, as it should have.

That big sin in the form of a stolen little poem etched in glass launched the trajectory of my relationship with Dad and his perception of me. Whether it began honestly or not, it happened, and now I'm glad for it because it led me here, to writing this book.

I look up at the November sky, far from the Signs of Spring, and whisper, "Thanks, Dad. And I'm sorry I cremated you."

ABOUT THE AUTHOR

Jaclyn Smith is a born storyteller with a gift for transforming life's most challenging moments into tales of resilience, humor, and grace. In her debut book, Jaclyn takes readers on a heartfelt journey through grief, family dynamics, and the unexpected solace she found in the world of improv comedy.

Growing up in Richmond, Virginia, and later in Marietta, Georgia, Jaclyn enjoyed a privileged childhood with loving and supportive parents. However, like many families, hers was not without its challenges. Generational trauma, illness, and anxiety wove their way through her formative years, shaping her experiences and perspectives. With a keen eye for detail and a compassionate heart, Jaclyn paints a nuanced picture of her family, acknowledging the beautiful moments alongside the difficult ones.

As an HR professional and former social worker, Jaclyn brings a unique understanding of the human experience to her writing. Her ability to connect with readers on a deep, emotional level is evident on every page of her book. Through her honest and relatable storytelling, she invites readers to explore their own family dynamics and find meaning in even the most trying circumstances.

One of the most striking aspects of Jaclyn's writing is her ability to find humor and light in the darkest of moments. When faced with the devastating loss of her father, Jaclyn turned to improv comedy as a means of coping and healing. Her journey into the world of improv not only helped her navigate her grief but also unlocked a new level of creativity and self-expression.

Jaclyn's debut book is a testament to the power of storytelling and the resilience of the human spirit. With her unique blend of humor, insight, and compassion, she has created a work that will resonate with readers from all walks of life. As her father always believed, Jaclyn is indeed a born writer, and her voice is one that the world needs to hear.

CONTACT

Jaclyn wants to share her insights and speak at your event, offering solace by reflecting on the caregiver or grief journey. Jaclyn is also available for book club events over Zoom or in person.

Please reach out and connect with her through her website, listed below. She's here to listen, support, and find the funny however she can.

WWW.JACLYNMICHELLESMITH.COM

Jaclyn Smith
JUN 19, 2022
02:08 PM

Veterans Victory House

Jaclyn Smith
JUL 03, 2022
02:44 PM

Jaclyn Smith
JUL 29, 2022
05:57 PM

Jaclyn Smith
JUN 26
09:50

Jaclyn Smith
JUL 24,
03:42

Jaclyn Smith
SEP 28, 2022
01:57 PM

Veterans Victory House

Jaclyn Smith
AUG 05, 2022
03:32 PM

Veterans Victory [House]

Jaclyn Smith
SEP 10, 2022
02:22 PM

Veterans Victory House

Jaclyn Smith
AUG 21, 2022
10:09 AM

Veterans Victor[y House]

Jaclyn Smith
SEP 20, 2022
12:49 PM

A115A
Veterans Victory House

Jaclyn Smith

OCT 22, 2022
11:17 AM

Veterans Victory House

Jaclyn Smith

NOV 04, 2022
05:06 PM

D125B

Veterans Victory House

Jaclyn Smith

OCT 30, 2022
11:11 AM

D125

Veterans Victory House

Jaclyn Smith

OCT 30, 2022
11:09 AM

D125B

Veterans Victory House

Jaclyn Smith
NOV 11, 2022
02:58 PM

Veterans Victory House

Jaclyn Smith
NOV 16, 2022
10:31 AM

D125B

Veterans Victory House

Jaclyn Smith
NOV 18, 2022
06:42 PM

D125B

Veterans Victory House

Jaclyn Smith
NOV 20, 2022
10:09 AM

D125B

Veterans Victory House

www.ingramcontent.com/pod-product-compliance
Lightning Source LLC
Chambersburg PA
CBHW030856170426
43193CB00009BA/629